GROWING UP
WESTERN

Monty Hall and Joe Durso, Jr.

Illustrated by R. F. Morgan

TWODOT

Helena, Montana

A · TWODOT · BOOK

© 1997 Joe Durso, Jr. and Monty Hall.
Illustrations ©1997 R. F. Morgan.
TwoDot is an imprint of Falcon Press® Publishing Co., Inc.
Helena and Billings, Montana

Design, typesetting, and other prepress work by Falcon Press, Helena, Montana. Cover and inside art by R. F. Morgan.

Printed in the United States of America.

Library of Congress Cataloging-in-Publication Data
Hall, Monty, 1930-
    Growing up western / Monty Hall and Joe Durso, Jr.
        p. cm.
    "A Twodot book"—T.p. verso.
    ISBN 1-56044-545-9
    1. Ranch life—Flathead River Valley (B.C. and Mont.)—Ancedotes.
2. Flathead River Valley (B.C. and Mont.)—Biography—Anecdotes.
3. Hall, Monty, 1930-   —Ancedotes. I. Durso, Joe, 1945-
II. Title.
F737.F6H34 1997
978.6'82033'092—dc21   96-7799
[B]   CIP

You can order extra copies of this book and get information and prices for other TwoDot books by writing to Falcon Press, P.O. Box 1718, Helena, MT 59624, or by calling 1-800-582-2665. Also, please ask for a free copy of our current catalog listing all Falcon Press books. To contact us via e-mail, visit our home page http: \\ www.falconguide.com.

Monty Hall dedicates his story to:

Brian and Tracy Hall,
who never gave their dad trouble as kids,
and make him proud as adults,

Laurie Hall,
1962-1986,
the kind of cowgirl Old Al would have liked,
and

Jo Ann Hall,
the finest woman God Almighty ever created,
who helped them grow up right.

Contents

Preface

This book was my wife Maureen's idea. We got to know Monty Hall because we frequently ate dinner at a good steak house in Stevensville, Montana, called the Fort Owen Inn. Monty Hall owned it during a brief escape from his toil as a cattle rancher.

Monty watched over his customers in the restaurant as he had tended new calves on his range. He greeted newcomers when they arrived, he made it a point to get to know them personally, and he roamed the dining room making sure everything was O.K. For regulars, he'd often buy a round in the lounge after dinner. And he loved to talk. Or "visit," as he'd say.

Turned out he was an engaging storyteller. Maureen and I would prompt him into recollections of his experiences during a lifetime on Montana ranches, and he always came to dwell on his growing-up years in the Flathead Valley during the

Depression and the two people who had raised him, his grandparents, Old Al and Ruth Ella Neas. They were pioneers in spirit and in fact. Old Al got his family through the toughest of times in some of the roughest of places, and he instilled in young Monty Hall a focus on survival that has carried into his adult life.

What emerged from numerous "visits" in Monty's restaurant turned out to be more than a series of intriguing and often funny after-dinner anecdotes. It seemed to Maureen and me that we were hearing a story about two things. On one level, Monty was recalling life on a small western Montana ranch during the 1930s—which was interesting enough. But on another level, he was talking about the origin of attitudes and how they direct our actions throughout our years. Specifically, he was telling us about the origin of a distinctly western attitude, a holdover from frontier times, an independent, self-sufficient, confident, arrogant attitude, with an unexpected underbelly of softness and thought.

After one especially funny or revealing session of storytelling in the bar of the Fort Owen Inn, Maureen exclaimed, "Monty, you should write a book!" I leaned into the conversation and said, "And I'll help you."

During the next two years, Monty Hall and I spent an enormous amount of time together. We drank last-night's coffee many early mornings in the empty dining room of his restaurant while I pumped him for more recollections and probed for deeper emotions, and his fat dog sniffed over the floor for spilled crumbs.

We traveled together to Big Bar Creek in British Columbia and found the house where Old Al and Ruth Ella raised ten kids and beat back the killer Spanish Flu of 1918. We tracked down and interviewed old folks, some of them in nursing homes, who had recollections of the Neas family, Kalispell during Prohibition, and some of the people and events in this book. Some of them requested anonymity, like the bootlegger who related his recipe for moonshine.

I spent hours in libraries, courthouses, and archives, reading old newspapers, court records, and reports from government agencies such as the Agricultural Extension Service. I visited the impressive Montana Historical Society in Helena and the tiny town museum in Clinton, British Columbia. Both contain amazing collections.

This research helped me understand and relate Monty's anecdotes in their context. The murder of Monty's Uncle Budd was a big deal in Kalispell in 1930, and it's still controversial there today. My reconstruction of the day of the murder comes from interviews with people I could find who were participants in the events of that day, accounts in local newspapers of what other people said, court documents and affidavits gathered by defense and prosecution, and records and correspondence of the Montana State Department of Corrections. The rifle Dogie Duncan used to kill Budd

Neas is in a storeroom at the Montana Historical Society.

Many of us in the television generations got our impression of how rural families survived the Great Depression from the popular show *The Waltons*. That series did not present a universal picture, of course. Young Monty Hall was a contemporary of the character John-Boy Walton, and he grew up in similar economic circumstances. But Monty's education about life was very different. Monty Hall was a kind of naughty John-Boy. (Monty says John-Boy was a "dink.") Monty's grandfather, Old Al, was a roguish Grandpa Walton. Both the real and the TV families got by.

We wanted to produce an accurate picture of life on a hardscrabble ranch in western Montana during the Depression. But our title, "Growing Up Western," is meant to denote more than geography. It's also about a philosophy of life and its genesis.

After a few years trying his hand as a restaurateur, Monty returned to his intended calling, babying cattle instead of customers. He lives with his wife, Jo Ann, on a ranch in Hot Springs, Montana.

I must thank some of the people who helped us prepare this book with their advice and their critiques. In addition to Maureen, they include most especially my father, Joe Durso, who was with us in many ways from chapter one. Also thanks to Charlie Hood, Gus Miller, Jack Saunders, Gregg Peterson, Jim Jordan, and Bob McGiffert. And a special nod to

Kay Ellerhoff, who forged the essential link between author and publisher, and to Megan Hiller, editor and advocate, who saw the same things in Monty's story that I did.

And most of all, I want to acknowledge the contribution of Joanna, my daughter, who as a young girl was willing to give up the soft life in a beautiful Chicago suburb to take a shot at growing up western.

Joe Durso, Jr.
Victor, Montana
October 14, 1996

Prologue

T hings got a little bit western the day the cowboys decided to hang the hippie after the rodeo in Niarada. This isn't the Old West we're talking about here. This occurred not too many years ago in a little town near the Flathead Valley in Montana. I was there, and so were my daughters, Laurie and Tracy. Laurie was fifteen, so she saw it all, but Tracy was younger and I wouldn't let her watch while they put the rope around the hippie's neck. Aside from everything else, the language the boys were using was pretty ripe for a kid to hear.

It started when we were all sitting around Todd Sanders' bar after the rodeo, letting the winners spend their prize money on drinks, and they were spending it well. Picture this real Montana bar with the sunlight of a late afternoon slanting through the windows forming pools on the floor, the place packed with men in hats and boots with their girlfriends and wives and their kids, most of them dusty and smudged from the day's events, tired and happy and loud, a lot of the men, and some of the women, getting pretty well loaded.

Outside were a couple dozen pickups and horse trailers, and horses tied and standing three-legged, many of them still with the saddles on their backs, patiently waiting to go home and get fed. Pick a summer weekend and you can see this scene all over Montana.

But the one thing out of place in Sanders' bar in Niarada that afternoon was the booth with the four hippies in it. I have no idea where they come from, but there they were, long hair and all, as strange in that setting then as a yuppie in a three-piece suit would be today.

At one point, Bill Finch sent his son out to check on the horses. The kid come back and whispered that he'd just seen one of them hippies taking the saddle off Lee Lytton's horse and putting it in the trunk of his car. Lee had already gone down the road and left his horse with Bub Borders to bring home, so Bub got up and looked over at the booth where the hippies were sitting. Then he walked over and stood in front of the one the kid had pointed out.

"I want to look in the trunk of your car," says Bub.

"No son-of-a-bitch looks in my trunk," says the hippie.

Old Bub reached out and grabbed a handful of long hair and just pulled that hippie out of the booth backwards and started for the door. The hippie was dragged along behind him, flapping his arms and scrabbling with his heels, trying to get his feet under him. Naturally, most of the cowboys trooped out after them, drinks in hand, to see what was going to happen.

Bub drug him up to the back of the car by his hair and says, "Now, open it!" and the hippie did, and there inside was Lee Lytton's saddle.

This must have been an especially stupid hippie, because what Lee was using that day was his special, personalized saddle, the one he'd had hand-made just for him by Earl Twist of Kalispell. It was all hand-tooled and had Lee's name stamped in the leather and everything. It was worth a lot of money, but when a thief went to sell it he'd raise eyebrows all over any pawn shop in Montana.

When those cowboys seen Lee's saddle in that hippie's trunk, they raised a hell of a ruckus, and one of them shouted, "Let's hang the bastard!"

Well, with all the booze they'd had, this seemed like one hell of an idea. So they got a couple of lariat ropes and tied them together and dragged this hippie over to the cross arm above the gate. By now, he's whiter than I'd ever seen a man and big-eyed, and when they threw the rope over the cross arm and put the noose around his neck and started to string him up, he messed his pants.

Now, when this started, they didn't intend to hang him to

death, at least I don't think they did. But they were sure going to stretch him long enough so he'd learn what it meant to come to a cowboy bar and steal a man's saddle. At least that's what I believe was the idea, but the way those boys were riled up, and with the liquor that had flowed, I wasn't real sure how it would end.

About the time we were going to find out, Todd Sanders came out of his bar. Todd is a big, tough man you just don't mess with. He walked up and pushed a couple of the boys away and took the rope off the hippie's neck, and he says to him, "You come with me!"

"What are you going to do with me?" croaks the hippie.

Says Todd, "I'm going to try to save your damn life!"

Todd had an old storeroom where he kept the beer and stuff, no windows, with a big, wooden door and a padlock. He shoved the hippie in there, hit the lock, and called the sheriff to come get him. To this day, I believe it's very likely that Todd Sanders did in fact save that hippie's life.

It's not that the men who were stringing him up were bad men, or unkind, or easily given to murder. Most of them even had their families there that day. But the crime they had discovered was an outrage by their code, and they reacted in a way that showed some characteristics of the lifestyle we had been brought up in. We preferred to handle problems ourselves, we wanted justice to be swift, and being rough was just a part of life. It was a lot like the time we sabotaged the irrigators' water supply.

I was ranching near Kila, a little community west of Kalispell in a beautiful little valley with Ashley Creek running through it. There were six of us small ranchers there along the creek, running some beef cattle and putting up hay to feed them. At least we were trying to put up hay.

The problem was, the dairy farmers about seven miles down the valley had water rights to Ashley Lake, an impoundment in the mountains at the head of our valley. To put it simple, we were between them and their water supply. Every spring, when they wanted to start irrigating their fields, they'd open up the head gate in the dam at Ashley Lake. The water they'd release would come boiling down Ashley Creek, overflow the banks, and flood us out. We'd have a hay meadow full of ripe green grass, but when it was ready for mowing, it would be under four inches of water.

There was a very simple solution to this problem. The irrigators could run their water from May until June when they put up their first crop of alfalfa. Then they could shut the water off for about three weeks so our fields would dry out and we could put up our grass hay. Then they could open the head gate again to irrigate their second crop. We were talking about our survival here, which they should have understood. Without hay put up, we'd have nothing to feed our cattle during the winter unless we bought hay, and who could afford that?

We asked them nice, real nice, several times. We even offered to put on extra crews of mowers and balers to put our crop up in a hurry so the water'd be off for the shortest time possible. There's no reason why this compromise wouldn't have worked for everyone. But those stubborn bastards downstream of us wouldn't budge. They wanted every drop of water they thought they were entitled to, whether they needed it or not, no matter who else it screwed. So, still trying to be good citizens, we took the problem before a judge.

The first day of the trial, Leo Molitor turns to me in the courtroom and says, "We're goin' to lose this case."

I says, "Why are ya sayin' that?"

He says, "Look at that judge. Look at the sandals that son-of-a-bitch is wearin'."

And sure enough, poking out from under that judge's robe were sandals, the kind with just a sole and leather straps on top.

Leo was a good judge of character, and he was sure as hell right this time. That judge eventually said the irrigators had every legal right to blow their water over the banks of Ashley Creek and flood our hay crop. But this just wouldn't do, don't you see? I had a family and three hundred mother cows to feed, and they were all depending on me. Have you ever stood in a field of beautiful grass hay, ankle deep in water, knowing you'll never get the hay up and that this might be the year you can't make it? If you have, you know why I and Leo took matters into our own hands.

We took some rough steel and cut it into wedges, a couple inches thick at the top, tapering down to a point. After dark, we went up to Ashley Lake and turned the wheel on top of the dam to crank the head gate down tight and shut off the water. Then we dropped the steel wedges point first down along the sides of the head gate in the channel it rode up and down on, and when the irrigators turned the wheel to open 'er up again, the wedges bound tight and they couldn't do it. They had a hell of a problem. They had to take everything apart to get them wedges out, and all this time, the water was shut off. And as soon as they'd get her working, we'd go up and wedge it shut again. We took turns going up there every night for several weeks, doing something or other to keep that water back, and that was the year we got our hay crop up.

Now what was wrong about that? Nobody lost anything. The irrigators below us got their first crop of alfalfa up before we shut them down, we got our own grass hay up for once, and then we let them irrigate some more. Sometimes you just need to do what you know is right, especially when you're responsible for the welfare of others. I felt the same way the time I built the hollow haystacks to fool the bankers.

I was managing a large ranch in Pleasant Valley for a man named Bob Elliott, a rich man who lived in California and also owned farms in the Midwest. He'd come out to Montana a couple of times a year, but aside from that I ran the place as if it were mine and I did it my own way.

This particular year, Elliott was trying to get a loan from an outfit in Salt Lake City to buy more cattle for the ranch, some four or five hundred head, so it was a pretty big deal. Any bank that has any sense at all will make sure a person has enough land and hay to feed the cattle before it loans him the money to buy them. They want their investment taken care of. Also, if you go belly-up and the bank has to repossess the cattle, they can repossess the hay to feed them, too. So Elliott had to demonstrate that he could produce enough hay to take care of these new cows along with the ones he already had.

The problem was, this year we had a little bit of a drought and the hay crop was short. I knew this was just a temporary condition, and that one way or another we'd make it through the winter, and next year would be fine. But I was sure as hell worried about convincing some pencil-pushing banker in Salt Lake City who'd maybe never seen a cow operation and didn't know there were ups and downs and that some years you had to make do and other years you were fat.

We put up much of our hay in huge sheds, big structures with just a roof supported by poles, no sides, and you could see exactly what was in them. We'd stack the hay in layers of about three hundred bales, and we could go twenty-one layers high, so each shed held a pile of hay. But this year, there wasn't enough hay to fill them to the top because of the drought, and I was worried about how this would look to the man the bank sent out to inspect the place.

So this time, we stacked the first sixteen layers like always. But for the top five layers we put one row of bales just around the outer edge, with nothing but air on the inside. From the outside, the whole stack looked perfectly normal. But the truth was, over the four sheds we had, I was really almost six thousand bales short. That's about two hundred tons of hay.

But my idea was for the bank's agent to go back and call the home office and tell 'em we had more hay than we'd ever need, that this was really some outfit, and they should go ahead and make the loan. So when this guy came out, I drove him around and he looked things over and nodded and off he went. Elliott got his loan, the next year the sheds were full for real, and everybody made out O.K. in the end, includin' the bank.

Sometimes, when you know something will work out if it just has a chance, it's up to you to make it happen.

Like these two friends of mine who had neighboring ranches and found themselves short of cattle about the time the bank agent was scheduled to come out and count the herd. The bank would do this once a year to make sure all the cattle it had loaned money on were in fact present. Well, these two guys had sold off some cows here and there because they needed money to make ends meet, and they were both going to come up way short when the count was made.

So, just before the bank agent was to visit one of the ranches, they drove a bunch of cows over from the other guy's place and mixed all the cattle together. The agent counted them up and left. Then they drove the combined herd over to the other fellow's ranch in time for the bank agent's visit there, and he counted them again. One reason this worked is that the bank employed at least one stupid agent at that time, and all he did was count heads, not check brands.

I thought this was a pretty slick piece of work. Of course, these two boys were taking advantage of a fact Charlie Russell had pointed out some time before: half of those bankers couldn't find their dad's milk cow if she was standing in the corral with a bell on.

Do you ever wonder where your attitudes come from? Do you ever wonder why you react under pressure the way you do, or where you got your ideas about the difference between right and wrong?

I built the hollow haystacks and spiked the irrigators' head gate without much thought, acting on instinct, you might say, or at least acting in a way that seemed quite natural. Like my neighbors who swapped cows at counting time, I was doing what was best for the people who depended on me, and along the way nobody got hurt, really. I considered it a matter of survival. When I look back on my life, I can see many occasions when this instinct, or whatever you want to call it, took over. And now that I'm older and have thought about this a bit, I know exactly where it came from.

I learned it from the man who raised me on a hardscrabble Montana ranch during the years of the Depression, my grandfather, the man I knew as Old Al.

My Friend Gyp

Old Al always said the first thing you do with a dog is treat it like a dog. That's why Gyp never got to come in the house, not even once, no matter what the weather. And Old Al never petted Gyp and didn't like other people petting her either, even me. He always said petting a horse or a dog just goofed them up. An animal, he said, man or beast, learns not by kindness, but by fear. This was a bit hard for me to deal with when I was little, because Gyp was my only friend.

Gyp was what they called an Australian Drover, medium sized, longish hair, and yellow-brown in color. She was one hell of a cow dog and she worked hard for Old Al. He'd go riding out to gather cows and she'd stay right by his horse's side until he saw some cow in the brush where the horse couldn't go. Then he'd say, "Gyp! Sissst! Sissst!" and he'd point and off she'd go, biting at the cow's heels. When she'd moved the cow to where Al wanted it, he'd shout "Back!" and back she'd come to the side of his horse.

Those Australians breed great cow dogs, all of them heelers, the Drovers like Gyp and the Australian Shepherds and the Blue Heelers. Folks around Kila got their Drovers from Coke Herman over in Niarada. Coke kept seven of them for himself and named them all Jack. He used to say, "You can holler 'Jack!' and one of 'em will be there, maybe all seven!"

Our Gyp was a great watchdog. She only barked when a person came on the place, never at a coyote or other animal, and when she barked Old Al got out of his chair and went to see what was up. Whenever someone visited our place, Gyp watched him like a hawk. She'd follow that person wherever he went, not making any sound, just watching. And as soon as he touched something, anything, Gyp would bite him. She done it every time unless Old Al made her stay by him.

One day when I was about five years old, I and Al were out in the cow barn milking, at least he was milking and I was thinking I was helping. Gyp started barking, and we went to the barn door to see what she had. Turned out it was a Maytag salesman. He says he wants to talk with the lady of the house.

Old Al asks, "What are ya sellin'?"

"Maytag washing machines," the guy answers.

"Well," says Old Al, shaking his head to the rhythm of his words, "I ain't got two dimes to rub together. There ain't no sense talkin' to her. We can't afford nothin' like that."

Then this Maytag guy says, "Perhaps you didn't understand. I said I'd like to talk with the lady of the house."

While this was going on, Gyp was just standing there watching him, real quiet. And I remember I noticed the ass of his pants. They were shiny, you know, like clothes get when you wear them too long. I noticed them for a couple of reasons. First, because they were dress pants, light blue slacks, which were a mighty rare sight on our place, and I thought they looked funny. I usually wore bib overalls or jeans, mostly with patches on them, and so did Al. The second reason I looked at this guy's ass is I knew what was coming.

Anyway, after this guy told Old Al that perhaps he didn't understand, Al looked at him for a beat or two and then said, "O.K., she's up at the house there."

The cow barn was set close to the county road, a ways from the house and a bit lower, and as this Maytag salesman walked up the trail with Gyp padding along behind him, Old Al says to me, "Watch this."

The guy went up on the porch and got in one knock on the door when Gyp nailed him. She took him right in the ass, high up on one cheek. She got some flesh and ripped them shiny blue pants right down one leg. I and Old Al started laughing, and Al says, "Guess we showed that son-of-a-bitch!"

Jeeze, that guy was mad. He come right back down, his pants leg dragging, blood on his hand where he'd checked his behind. By now, Old Al had picked up a pitchfork from somewhere, and he's leaning on it. The Maytag guy storms up to him and says, "I'm gonna sue you! You'll hear from my attorney! I'm gonna have the sheriff out here! I'm gonna have that dog killed!"

Old Al says, "Nooo. The only thing you're gonna do is get the hell off of this ranch."

And he did, and we never heard nothing more about it.

I'd been living with Old Al and Grandma for four years by then. They got me when I was thirteen months old, in 1932, almost a year and a half after the murder of my uncle Budd. By then Grandma had been grieving so long and so hard her nerves were all shot, and Old Al thought he was going to have to dig Budd up so she could look at him one more time. For a while he thought he'd have to send her away someplace, she was that bad off. Then I came along. Grandma always said I was a Godsend, because my arrival snapped her out of it and gave her someone to focus all that emotion on. The fact that I looked like Budd helped, too.

My mother was Bell Bernice Neas, the fifth child of Grandma and Old Al. Everybody called her Bernie, except Grandma, who called her "Burniss," which rhymed with "furnace." Nobody ever talked about what had happened between her and Mark Hall, the logger who was my father, but there she was one day in 1932 at age twenty-two, back home with a baby and no money to support him. But my mother was a woman full of pride, and there was no way she'd move in and mooch off of Old Al and Grandma. So I got dropped off, and Mom went to Kalispell to work in a WPA sewing room.

I would see her from time to time when she'd come out to the ranch for a visit, and occasionally I'd spend a night with her in Kalispell. She lived in a little cabin in town that had one room downstairs and a little kitchen, and one room upstairs. I remember lying in bed with her one night and noticing that she'd papered the walls and the underside of the roof with newspaper. She was barely getting by and had no money for wallpaper, but at least what she'd put up made the place clean.

Somehow she managed to get enough money together to buy me the only new toys I ever got when I was a kid, a red wagon and a Shooting Star sled. She dragged that wagon three and a half miles through deep snow so I'd have it on Christmas morning, and she always made sure I had warm clothes to keep out the winter cold. And she never said one negative word about my father.

I never saw him until I was thirteen and he came to visit. Grandma wrote him a letter at one point and asked him to help support me, because times were so tough and they were broke. He sent her ten dollars, and that was the extent of his child support. I guess times were tough for him, too. He did send me a pair of skis once when I was little, and I thought that was great.

"A warm winter coat would sure in hell be better then them skis," was Grandma's response to this generosity. "His ass is bare and what does he do? He sends him skis! He don't need skis! He needs a winter coat!"

But one way or another, I always had a winter coat.

My earliest memories are of growing up on the Kjos place, a little one-hundred-and-sixty-acre ranch near Smith Lake that Old Al rented. When I arrived, the household included Florence and Gladys, who were teenagers and would be leaving home soon, and Leslie, the first child, who was retarded from birth and would never leave. And there was Old Al's brother Andrew, who lived with them when he wasn't off on some ranch job somewheres. So that little place was bursting at the seams when I showed up.

Old Al ran cattle and raised horses and kept a small dairy herd, and they did whatever they could to make a buck here and there. Grandma's main contribution was her turkeys.

She must of had a hundred of them running loose around the house. Every Thanksgiving and Christmas, she and Old Al would butcher some and sell them to Eddie Nordtome, who owned a meat market in Kalispell. Old Al would hang them by their feet and then drive a curved knife up into their brains to kill them and loosen their feathers at the same time. If you just chop off a turkey's head his feathers don't loosen and you tear his skin up trying to yank them out. With a chicken, now, you can chop him and then scald him in water to loosen the feathers, but that don't work with a turkey. You gotta stab him right in the brain, then those feathers all come loose.

So Grandma had all these turkeys running around the place and she had a nice shed for them to nest in and lay their eggs. But every once in a while one of them old bitches would decide the shed wasn't good enough and she'd sneak off and make her nest somewhere out of sight. The problem with this was she'd likely lose half her brood to skunks and dogs and whatever, and this was cash money we're talking about losing. So one of my assignments was tracking the renegade turkeys and saving their eggs.

You can tell when a turkey is about to break away. When Grandma would feed them, she'd throw some grain out on the ground and they'd mill around and peck. Pretty soon, there'd be a hen who'd start to take off. She'd act like she don't even know where she's going. She'd walk off over there for a bit, and next thing you know, she headed over here, but all the time she's getting further away. She'd be a-picking and scratching, but she's watching you all the time.

There was this one old bitch that had wandered off like this and had a nest somewhere, and Grandma told me to find it. I followed her for three days when she'd head off for her nest, and I couldn't stay with her. She'd go across the county road and get into this little bunch of timber and disappear. I'd creep along after her, laying down so she wouldn't see me, and then she'd go over some little hill and I'd stand up and she'd be gone.

Those turkeys will just sit there on their nest and crouch down, and you can walk two feet away from them and they won't move. I really hated following them sons-of-bitches, and I was really mad at this one—three damn days wasted. But Grandma had said to find that nest, so I had to do it.

Finally I found her. She was behind some old logs. She'd walk along and come up to those logs and just hop over them and be gone. But I got her. She had about half a dozen eggs on the nest, and she'd go back every day and lay another one or two. I brought all of them home but one, which I left on the nest so she'd keep laying there. When she was done laying and got ready to set, I brought them all in.

Meanwhile, Grandma'd been keeping the eggs I was bringing home in the house. She put an "x" on them, and every day she'd turn them over, just like a turkey will do, so the baby chick doesn't stick to one spot on the inside of the shell. One day, the "x's" would be up, the next day they'd be down, and Grandma would do this until that old hen was ready to set. Once a turkey's ready to set, she don't care where it happens, so Grandma would put the eggs in a nest in the shed where they belonged.

Those damn turkeys were useless as far as I was concerned, but they turned out to be good for one thing. When I was little, I wanted to be just like Old Al, and one of the things I wanted to learn how to do was use a rope. He was so good at it, and he taught me, and told me I could rope all the fence posts I wanted. That was fine for a while, but wasn't very exciting after I got so I could do it regularly. So those turkeys were in trouble.

Their long necks were just right, sticking up there, and I'd sail that loop out and over their heads and jerk it tight. They'd squalk and flap around and make a great commotion, and I had a fine time until Grandma caught me and put an end to that. But I'd still do it from time to time when I knew she was gone.

It was sometimes hard for a little kid to find ways to amuse himself when there weren't other kids around, and I wasn't really being bad or doing something I knew was hurtful to the turkeys, just like I wasn't trying to be mean to the chickens when I dunked them in the sour milk.

Old Al would separate all the milk he got from his dairy cows, so he wound up with cream and skim milk. The cream he'd sell, and the skim milk he'd feed to the calves. Those calves would have done better on whole milk, but selling cream was a source of steady cash year-round, and Al had to make a dollar any way he could. The calves might grow a little slower, but they grew, and it was just one of those compromises he had to make.

Anyway, the calves couldn't drink up all the skim milk, so

what was left Old Al dumped in a wooded barrel by the barn. There it sat, souring in the hot sun. It got all clabbered and lumpy and smelly. The barrel was covered with a piece of tin, and it was hot inside, and got to be really disgusting. When Old Al fed his pigs, he'd dump some of this clabbered milk on their food, and they really ate it up.

I was bored one day when I was about five and looking for something to do when I seen these chickens. We kept chickens for the eggs and also to eat, and there they were, walking around the barnyard, minding their own business. I caught one up by the feet and dunked her down in that barrel of clabbered milk, and then I turned her loose. Her feathers were all soaked and her wings were heavy and she spread them out and staggered around trying to get her balance. It looked so silly I caught up several more and dunked them in.

Pretty soon there was a bunch of milk-logged chickens stumbling around the barnyard, and I thought that was the funniest thing I'd ever seen. I was dunking chickens and turning them loose and laughing my head off when Old Al came up.

"You think that's funny, don't you?" he asked.

"Yeah!" I replied. "Look at 'em!"

He didn't answer. What he did was grab me by the scruff of the neck and push my head down in the barrel. I went all the way under, deep into that sour, rotten, stinking milk. It went in my ears and lumps of it went up my nose, and then he released me. I ran crying to Grandma, who cleaned me up, and after that the chickens got a break.

That was a wonderful place to grow up, that little ranch, and I never really knew how tough it was for them to get by. There wasn't enough money for toys and I didn't have other kids to play with, but since that was all I knew I never felt deprived of anything.

In fact, I felt lucky in a way because I had Grandma to love me, and I always knew Mom was out there, too, so I had two women in my life. And then there was Old Al.

He was over sixty years old when Mom dropped me off, and his hair was white. He had raised ten children of his own and buried a son. He got up at four o'clock every morning, no matter what the season, and he struggled to earn a living for himself and to provide for his family as he had always done, and now he had me on his hands. But busy as he was, he never seemed to mind that. In fact, he seemed to sense that I needed some kind of companionship, so he set aside a small portion of every day just for me.

Grandma insisted that I take a nap every afternoon, whether I was tired or not, but there was a little time between lunch time and nap time when I got to play. I'd come up to the front door and knock. He'd open it and exclaim, "Well for Christ's sake, Monty, how are ya!" and he'd invite me in. I'd call Grandma Mrs. Neas, and tell them how I'd come over from Marion where I lived, how I'd taken my son Marvin to school ahorseback that morning when it was eighty below, and he'd go along with all this, and so would Grandma.

He'd sit there in his high-backed kitchen chair smoking a cigarette, and he always crossed his legs. I'd sit in a chair opposite him, puffing on a licorice cigarette he'd brought home from Kila for me. But I was mad because I couldn't plant one foot and cross my legs like he could, the chair being too tall. So Old Al fixed that. He cut the legs off my chair until it was just right. Grandma was really unhappy about this because we didn't have that many chairs to begin with, but Old Al knew just what it would take to make my small life complete, so he done it, and every day before my nap we'd sit there with our legs crossed, smoking.

And then, of course, there was Gyp.

She was my constant playmate when we lived on our rented ranch near Kila, this dog Gyp, Old Al's cow dog. She was very tolerant of the games little kids like to play, and let me hang several kinds of harnesses off her. She pulled my red wagon in the summer and my sled in the winter, and when I'd seen Al skidding logs with his team, Gyp became a draft horse and we pulled sticks out of the woods.

She also liked to chase cats and I liked to watch her do it, so the cats on our place got a good workout. There were plenty of cats around, too. Old Al always said, "Twenty cats are better'n one mouse!" So he just let them breed and hang out in the barn. Nothing like a cat got spayed or neutered on our place in those days, so these cats just kept multiplying and pretty soon there was more of them than one small ranch needed, but that seemed to be O.K. with Old Al. I remember he used to tell me, "Don't feed them barn cats! They'll stop catchin' mice!" So I didn't feed them, but when it got cold out, he'd give them some milk and other stuff. A bunch of them would die over the winter, but that was fine, because come spring there'd be a whole new crop of kittens to take their place.

Anyway, Gyp loved to chase those cats and I was all for it. She never did it while Al was there because he'd of whipped her ass, and she never did it on her own because a good cow dog won't chase after anything unless told to. But I'd take Gyp out cat hunting when Grandma and Old Al weren't around. We'd find some cat and I'd shout, "Take 'em out, Gyp!" which is one way Old Al would set the dog after some cow. Gyp would hear my small voice yell that, and off she'd go, and off would go the cat. Gyp never failed to run them cats down, and when she got them, she killed them.

I remember one cat in particular that made a notable effort to get away. She tried to escape up the side of Old Al's hay shed. She was climbing like mad up a six-by-six square post, but she couldn't get a good enough grip on the wood with her claws. Gyp leaped up and nailed her and dragged her down and killed her dead, and I applauded and cheered and Gyp smiled and looked mighty pleased.

Gyp would chase after anything I put her onto. I'd let her chase the milk cows when I went out to bring them in, though not enough so their tongues were hanging out and Old Al'd notice. One day, I sent her after a big, black, workhorse mare that Al had. He was away and didn't see this episode, fortunately. I started Gyp after the horse in a pasture up near the house, and Grandma recalled hearing my young cry of glee, "Weeee, look at 'em go, Grandma!"

Pretty soon, Gyp had run the horse behind a row of willows and into the back pasture where I couldn't see them, so I went on to other amusements. Several days later, Old Al found his workhorse dead in the stream that run along the edge of the back pasture, six feet deep.

I remember hearing him tell Grandma, "I *cannot* imagine why that horse went all the way in there."

It was hard to understand, as none of the animals went near the stream because it was surrounded by a real nasty bog that would trap a horse or a cow. If they went in there, they'd get stuck good and not be able to get out without help, and they knew it. I couldn't imagine why the horse would do that, either.

But Grandma knew. Years later she told me she was sure the horse had run right into the creek after I'd set Gyp on her, and there she'd got stuck. Grandma also told me she never let on to Old Al what she suspected.

So Gyp was my reliable playmate in the innocent games

of a small child, and in mischief as well. And when it was time for me to go to first grade she performed a really important service.

To get to the bus stop, I had to walk about a mile and a half, and the first part of it was down a lane with trees pressing on both sides. I had to leave the house real early, and in winter it was awful dark. Gyp would walk along with me until the road broke out of the trees. Then I'd say, "O.K., Gyp," and she'd turn back and head for home.

It's not that I was afraid, really. Old Al never let anybody be afraid. He simply wouldn't permit it. He never permitted anybody to tell me ghost stories to try to spook me, like my cousins would try to do on the rare times they came out to visit from town. He'd put a stop to it right away. One day one of "them damn town kids" was telling me not to go outside at night because there was bats that would get in your hair, vampire bats that would suck your blood. Old Al jumped on him right away.

"You're so fulla shit it's runnin' out your ears," he said, "That's all bullshit." He'd talk to a little kid just like that.

So I wasn't afraid to walk down that road in the dark at age six—wasn't allowed to be—but somehow I felt better when Gyp came along. She was such a good pal in so many ways, I felt really crummy the day I almost got her killed.

I was about five when my cousin Rusty Burnett, a "damn town kid," came out from Kalispell to visit for a day. We were playing in Old Al's hay shed, which was full of hay, and up on top we found where one of Grandma's chickens had made a nest. It had about half a dozen eggs in it. This Rusty picked one up and chucked it at a post and busted it. Now, I knew this was wrong, but I went along with it anyway, and we broke all them eggs against the post. That evening when he went out to feed, Old Al found them.

"Who broke them eggs?" he asked at supper.

I paused a second, then said, "Gyp, she done it."

"You sure it was her?"

"Yeah, she done it."

He got up from the table and went and got the rifle.

"What are ya gonna do?" Grandma asked.

"I'm gonna go kill that dog," Al replied.

Well, that got the truth outta me in a hurry. If Old Al was running a bluff, it sure worked. Grandma chewed me out real good, but Old Al was willing to blame the whole thing on Rusty, the town kid, which seemed fair to me since he'd thrown the first egg.

Gyp was my constant companion on that ranch, and she played with me faithfully and put up with a lot. I never wondered about not having other kids for friends because I'd never known any other way to live. Gyp was there for me every day in the years before I went to school, and she walked me down the dark road to the first grade. It was a major sadness in my life when she was killed the following summer.

Old Al was moving some cattle along the road near Kila, and Gyp was helping him. There's a railroad track that runs along that road, and every once in a while a speeder would go by. A speeder is one of those little carts with a motor on it that the rail crews used when they were working on the line. Gyp liked to chase them. She never chased a car, but she'd chase speeders.

This time she got on the other side of the track from Old Al, and when she tried to come back she cut in front of the speeder. She wasn't quick enough and got run over. The only thing Old Al said about it when he got home for supper that night was, "Gyp got killed today."

Usually when an animal died on our place he'd just drag it off into the woods where the coyotes would dispose of the carcass pretty quick, there not being time, energy, or interest to do anything more ceremonial.

But this day, Al went back with a shovel and dug a hole near where Gyp had died and laid her in it. This cow dog he never once let in the house, never once petted, is the only animal I remember Old Al ever burying.

Nina's Horse

I stole my first horse when I was four.

It was a big old gelding eating grass along the county road, and it seemed the most natural thing in the world for me to lead him home. I took the laces out of my shoes, tied them together, draped them around his neck when he put his head down to eat, and led the gentle old thing to the barn on the place where we were staying and put him in a stall. Then I went in to see Grandma.

"Got me a horse," I announced.

"That's nice, son," she replied, not looking up from her kitchen work.

Sometime later, she glanced out the window and saw this horse's head sticking out the top door of the stall. That got her attention. She lit out of that house, grabbed the horse, and hustled him back to the roadside where people often turned their animals loose to graze along the edge. Then she told me never to do *that* again.

Ever since I can remember, I wanted to be a cowboy. Old Al had me up on a horse when I was two, and what else was there for me to be? The only people who came to the ranch to visit were guys like Coke Herman, L. G. Herman, Fred Huggins, and Chuck Jennings—good cowboys, just real, real good at what they did. I looked up to all of them and admired them, I suppose, like a kid looks up to a football star today. That old Chuck Jennings was a hell of a bronc rider, and I'd sit around listening while they told stories about rodeos and how the crowd went wild. There was so much glory in it.

I grew up around horses and was never afraid of them like some people are. Well, I was afraid only once that I can remember. Old Al had just weaned this colt, and had put him in a corral. He handed me the mare's halter rope and told me to take her into the barn and tie her up.

I was just five years old, and this was a great big mare, real tall. Her colt had just been taken away for the first time, and she was upset about it. She wasn't broke to ride or anything like that, just a halter-broke brood mare, and that colt was nickering, and the mare was whinnying and trying to pull away from me. I told Old Al I was afraid.

"You're *afraid*?" he said. "If you can't lead that horse to the barn, then gimme that rope and *I'll* lead her in. *You* go in the house and crawl under Grandma's *skirts*! And suck on her *tit* while you're under there!"

Boy, that made me mad. I jerked that horse's head around and led her into the barn and tied her up. I was scared all the time I was doing it, but I done it.

But I sure loved to ride. The only problem was there were just big horses around, no ponies, and they were hard for me to climb up on when I was little. And when I'd fall off, it was a long ways to the ground. One day I asked Old Al how come I couldn't stay on better.

"Your ass is too round," he said.

Later he saw me walking across the yard looking over my shoulder and feeling my rear to see just how round it was.

Another time when I was older I asked him how come I couldn't ride as good as him and my uncle Howard, and he gave me an answer that was probably closer to the truth.

"You had the wrong sire."

Whatever, I was determined to be a rider, I mean a really good rider, and my prospects took a giant leap one day when I was five and Old Al led Gypsy home.

Gypsy was a half-Shetland pony, just the right size for me to hop on with no trouble, and I don't think I was ever happier in my life than when he handed me the rope and said, "I got you a horse." The only problem was Gypsy's true ownership was a bit cloudy.

Old Al had got her from Plumis Moore, who lived with his family a ways down the road from us. Plumis was a logger, and Al had skidded some logs out of the woods for him with his teams—worked for him for quite some time—and Plumis owed him sixty dollars. Plumis never got his money out of the logs or bought something for himself with it. Al never got paid. Plumis would say, "Yeah, Al, yeah, I'll get ya paid one of these days."

Well, Old Al was up at their place one day and there was this little gray pony standing there. Al says to Plumis, "How 'bout me takin' her down for Monty to ride for a while?"

Old Plumis, he's trying to get along, so he says, "Yeah, go ahead."

Gypsy actually belonged to Plumis's daughter, Nina, who was about seven, and she was really pissed that I was riding her pony. When Plumis came to get it back, Old Al told him, "Sure, you can have the mare. Soon as you give me that sixty dollars." Al didn't get the sixty dollars, so Nina lost her horse.

Then one day this other man showed up and wanted the mare. He said Plumis had never paid *him* for it and he was taking her. Old Al said, "No, you are not," and run him off the place. All this debate frightened me sufficiently that I hid Gypsy in the back pasture out of sight of the county road whenever I turned her out. I was afraid someone was going to snatch my new horse away.

But Gypsy's previous "owners" had made a fundamental mistake: they hadn't branded her. Old Al took care of that. He branded an "N" on her shoulder and said, "I guess we know who owns her now."

Old Al came up with an old English saddle for me to use, but I didn't like it because he took the stirrups off it. I was always riding off alone, and he didn't want me to get hung up and dragged if I fell off. So I figured out something that was even more dangerous.

I'd saddle her up, and then when he wasn't looking I'd sneak into the barn and take two halter ropes and stuff them down my pants. When I'd ridden out of sight of the house, I'd put loops in the ropes and hang one off each side of the saddle for stirrups, an arrangement that would hang me up real good if I went off. But I didn't like that English saddle anyway, so I rode bareback most of the time.

Gypsy opened up a whole new world for me. I could go places now, and I went everywhere. I was on that little horse all day every day, and there wasn't a time that Old Al left the place ahorseback that I wasn't tagging along. If he said, "Well, I've got to ride up here and check on this," well, I was ready, and I mean right now.

We rode the hills together, me and Al, an old man and a five-year-old kid, him raisin' me as best he could after he'd raised ten of his own, him on big, black Rocky Tom and me on my little gray pony. The summer days were long and full of marvelous sights, like the range horses and their colts out there doing their thing, and all the while I was learning so much.

I remember one time we were hunting a bunch of horses

that Al had turned out. It was a big area we were looking in, and we checked all the likely springs and found nothing.

"Well," said Al, "they're up on top. I thought we might find 'em down to water."

We rode clear to the top of this ridge, and there they were, the whole damn bunch. They were all up there. I asked him how come, as hot as it was, they weren't down by the spring. He said in a hot summer like we were having they'd often go up on top where the flies weren't so bad, and that's just what they were doing, standing around in the shade, grazing. They'd come down to drink, then go right back up away from the flies.

One other time when I was some older we went up Dower's Draw to get a horse he wanted out of a bunch. We were listening for the bell mare, an old sow named Flame. Al'd hung a big bell around her neck, and when we went looking for the herd, we'd locate them by the sound of the bell. Well, of course, she'd lost the clapper out of it.

We found them eventually, up high, and started them down. When you first come on a bunch of horses or cattle and start them moving, they'll run, trying to get away from you. They'll make one good run until they're winded, then you can handle them. Both horses and cows will do that, but horses will run harder, and these sure did. Old Al had told me they were really going to come down off that ridge, but he said to just hang in there. They run clear away from us, down through the timber where we couldn't see, and suddenly there was silence.

We sat there listening to the quiet for a minute, then suddenly Al whirled his horse around and said, "Come on!"

"They're down below," I said, "they gotta be!"

He said, "No, they're not! Old Flame has pulled a switch on us!"

He was right. That old bitch had run ahead until she and the bunch were out of sight, then she'd made a circle and led them back up behind us. But she couldn't outfox Old Al. We found them again, and those horses had had their run, so we got them.

That Rocky Tom loved to chase other horses. They'd start up and he'd get all excited and want to go. I liked to watch him and Old Al come off of them hills, Al with his hat pulled way down, horses a-runnin' hard through the brush and timber, crashing through with no mind to what was under foot or coming up ahead, and I got to where I could do it just as good.

That was when I was older, of course, and riding the big horses. But my pony Gypsy was all the horse a little kid needed, and she never let me down. But she was part Shetland pony, remember, so I had to figure her out sometimes. People think Shetland ponies are mean. They're not mean. They're just smart, smarter'n hell, and they know how to handle a kid.

For example, if I wanted to gallop Gypsy away from home, she'd run just so fast and no faster, no matter what I did. Going toward home was a different story.

Well, they had this horse race for kids at the school picnic when I was in the second grade, and Noel Kaiser thought he had a pretty hot horse named Pet. I didn't think his horse was so hot, but damn it, every time we raced, me and Gypsy came in dead last—every single time. Noel's really enjoying this and giving me a lot of shit. And all the fathers there who knew the Neases always had good horses are snickering among themselves about how Monty's getting beat. Then I figured it out.

The way they'd set this course up, Gypsy was running *away* from home. So I proposed to Noel that we do one more race, and I picked a new starting point and a new finish line that had Gypsy pointed *toward* home. I got me a switch from a willow bush and warmed her up real good, and then off we went.

Gypsy outrun 'em all. Noel was astonished and wanted to go again, so we did, just I and him, and I whipped him again.

That night on the way home I had to ride past the road that led to Plumis Moore's place, and Nina was waiting for me. She grabbed Gypsy by one rein and she said, "I'm takin' my horse home."

The other of my bridle reins was a piece of an old drive line from a wagon rig, and it had a big snap on it that attached it to the bit. This was a big, heavy snap from a workhorse harness, and I reached down and undone it from the bit. I brought it up on the end of a little bit of slack line and I smacked Nina right across the face with it. She screamed and let go of the horse, and me and Gypsy took off. I only had one rein hooked up now, but it didn't matter, because Gypsy was headed for home and knew just where we were going.

When we got back, I told Old Al what had happened and what I'd done.

"Well," he said, "that was the thing to do."

We'd bred Gypsy, and that spring she had a colt. In the fall, after it was weaned, Old Al led it over to Moore's place and gave it to Nina.

Budd's Trunk

One day in the fall of 1938, Old Al came home with some news that would change our lives for the better—only he didn't know it when he walked in the door.

"He wants to sell that place," he told Grandma.

The "he" was Willis March, owner of the big dude ranch outside of Kila, but more important for us, owner of some land on the other side of Smith Lake from the Kjos place where we lived. "That place" was the site of the old March and Henderson lumber mill, a business started by Willis's father. It had burned down once, been rebuilt, and finally closed some years before. What was left was the building that had housed the offices, a barn, an outhouse, some other small buildings, a railroad siding, and the 160 acres of pasture that surrounded it. Old Al always thought it would make a hell of a ranch.

"He wants twelve hundred dollars for it," he continued. "But it would take four hundred dollars down. There ain't no way in hell we can do it." And he seemed resigned to staying put on the rented place where we were scratching out our living.

Grandma didn't say nothing. She just went into their bedroom and pulled Budd's trunk out from under the bed.

I'd heard her talking about Budd as long as I can remember. One time when I was little I asked her, "Well, where's he at?"

"He's in heaven," she replied.

"Well, when's he comin' back?" I asked, and she started crying.

That kind of got to me, and I knew that Budd was special to her and that his trunk was special, too. I remember it was a big green trunk, and as I grew older I came to realize that it was a sacred thing, something nobody opened, or even thought of touching, other than Grandma. I don't believe any of us would of even moved it.

In it she kept things that were really important to her, pictures and some things of Budd's, including the clothes he'd been wearing when he'd been killed with the bullet hole in the back of the shirt. She'd washed the clothes and kept them in the trunk slid under her bed.

When she went in there the day Old Al brought home the news about the March place, I followed her. She brought out the trunk, opened it, and took out a big can of talcum powder.

It was a big, round, pink can with flowers on it. She popped off the tin lid and dug down deep into that powder, pulled out a large wad of paper money, and peeled off some bills.

Then she went out to Old Al and handed him four hundred dollars.

"For God's sake," he said, "where'd you get that?"

"It doesn't matter where I got it," she replied. "There ya are."

I don't remember Old Al saying "thank you" or anything like that, but I do remember him saying something like, "Goddamn, this is great," and off he went to join the ranks of the landowners once again.

We moved over in the early spring, a team of horses pulling our belongings on a sled across the snow-covered fields that bordered Smith Lake. Our new home wasn't much, but it was a great leap upward from the Kjos place for each of us.

There was a nicer "house" than the one we'd been living in, but not by much. There were three rooms in the old lumber mill office building where we'd live—three rooms plus the vault room where'd they'd kept the money and whatever else they felt needed to be secure. But the big thing for Grandma was that it was right across the county road from the little "town" of Kila, which consisted of a school, a post office, a community hall, and Branch's Store. For the first time, she wasn't so isolated.

Neither was I. We now lived in "civilization," and I could

have friends over to play easily and I could go visit them. But for me there was one enormous improvement. I'd have my own room.

On the Kjos place I'd slept in the living room on a cot, and when I was real little and it was cold outside I'd slept in bed with Grandma and Old Al. But now, they assigned the vault to me. It was to be my room, mine, my sanctuary, and for this eight-year-old kid it was a tremendous advance in life.

This vault was about ten feet by twelve feet, and the walls were solid brick, nearly three feet thick, brick inside and out, and for some reason, they'd made the roof round, like a dome. There were four steel rods across the room at the top of the walls to bind the whole thing together, and I used to swing on them. That was one solid room, no way in but the door when it was used as a vault, but the people who'd rented the place before we bought it had cut two windows through the brick, so now some light got in.

But by God, that brick room was cold in the winter. The heat never made it down the hall from the main part of the house. At night Grandma would put a hot-water bottle or a flatiron under the covers to start me off warm, but in the morning I'd have to bail my ass out of bed and go like hell to the stove to dress.

The whole house was just a little bit warmer than the corral, for that matter. There was no insulation, naturally. Old Al "heated" the place with a wood stove made of two fifty-five-gallon drums, one on top of the other. He'd feed wood into the lower drum, and the stovepipe came out the back and wound through the upper one before it went on up and out. That was supposed to distribute the heat better. There was many a time when he got those barrels glowing red.

Old Al made one major improvement to the place. He put on a new kitchen. Him and his brother Andrew found a lot of railroad ties left behind when the lumber mill closed down, lots of untreated ties they'd made but never sold, and they gathered them together and built a huge room with them, stacking them like you would logs for a log cabin and spikin' them together. This kitchen ran the length of the house. It must have been thirty feet long, and all of its walls were railroad ties.

He also found some piles of shiplap siding lying around, and tore some more of it off one of the few real good buildings on the place, and he nailed it up on the inside of this new room so it would be nicer for Grandma. Into that new kitchen went her Majestic wood-burning cook stove, which we'd hauled across the snow on the sleigh. It had a big reservoir on one side that held water that was always hot. Grandma was really set up now.

And what did Old Al get out of this move for himself? For one thing, he got a good barn.

In fact, it was a great barn, some twenty-four feet by sixty feet, with stalls below and a full hayloft above. The barn on the Kjos place was such a tumble-down affair, this must have seemed to him as big a deal as my own room was to me. Only thing was, it was so full of shit he couldn't drive the team in the door.

The hames on their harness would bump against the top of the door and the horses couldn't get through. Hames are the part of a workhorse harness that stick upright over the withers. You attach the tug lines to them. These horses would bow their heads and try to get through the door, but the shit was piled so high they couldn't make it.

There must have been three feet of manure hardened there in that barn, and Old Al had to dig it out with a pick. Then he spread it over his new pastures to enrich the soil.

The other thing Old Al got out of the move was the opportunity to expand his farming. The Kjos place was plastered up against the hills, but it had the advantage of being adjacent to the grazing land Old Al leased up on top, so he could just turn his stock loose. After the move, he had to trail them to that range. But on the Kjos place, there hadn't been much open land to grow anything on.

The move to the ranch at Kila solved that problem, and Al set about planting grain, barley and rye, maybe fifty or sixty acres of it, and that allowed him to get back into the pig business.

He'd always kept some hogs around for the family to use,

butchering two or three a year. But now that he could grow grain for feed like he did when the family lived in British Columbia, he could raise hogs commercially, and in those days any new opportunity for cash was a big deal. He kept about ten sows, and they'd have as many as a dozen little pigs apiece, so we're talkin' about a significant new source of income here.

He rigged up a scale out by the pig shed, and he let everyone weigh their own pig. He trusted them all, except the preacher who showed up one day.

Old Al never really liked preachers, and when this one showed up he turned to me and said, "That's one of them Bible-packin' bastards. You go 'round and read that scale. I don't trust that son-of-a-bitch."

If you'd of come there to buy a pig, he'd of let you weigh it yourself and he'd of taken your word, but he sent me around to read the scale alongside the preacher.

So with the move off the Kjos place to that little ranch at Kila, Old Al was starting to do good again. He was raising horses and had his herd of cattle, and now he was back in the pig business. He was selling cream every day, and Grandma had her turkeys, which she sold at Thanksgiving and Christmas, and there was the garden and the milk cows and the chickens for our own use. We were on the verge of being a lot better off, and then Old Al found out about the back taxes that were owed on the place.

They amounted to three hundred dollars. Grandma got out Budd's trunk once more and dug down into that talcum powder can, and came up with half of it. My Uncle Howard came up with the other half somehow, and they paid off the back taxes. Then Old Al got ahold of Willis March, who was in California at the time, and they had a little chat about the situation.

Willis allowed as how the taxes really had been his responsibility, and to make up for the money Old Al and Howard had shelled out he proposed that they go up to his dude ranch and cut out twenty unbroken horses. He figured they could sell them for fifteen dollars apiece, and that way they'd get their three hundred back.

That was O.K. with Al, so one day I and him and Howard rode up to the dude ranch. Old Van Vorhees was taking care of it while Willis was away, and he watched us while we corralled fifty or sixty horses. Then Old Al got out his rope.

"You're just supposed to take unbroke horses," yelled Van Vorhees.

"Right," said Old Al, and he snaked his rope out and over the head of a real pretty little sorrel gelding. Then right away he flipped a coil of rope at the horse's face and it jumped back, of course.

"Yup, he ain't broke," yelled Van Vorhees when he seen the horse jump. "You can take him."

So Old Al and Howard kept doing this, and by the time

they'd picked out twenty they had a good number in the bunch that were, in fact, broke to ride just fine, including that sorrel horse. Grandma named him Redwing, and I rode him around the place for several days. I really wanted to keep him, too, but Old Al sold him right away for sixty dollars.

That's also how he got his two great mares, Charlemagne and Chocolate, both of them also broke to ride, and he bred them both for a lot of years and made his tax money back several times over.

So this move to Kila finally got us on a little better economic footing, and you could see it if you looked close. It meant that I got new jeans more often, although Grandma still patched them when they tore. And I got new shoes from time to time, instead of having to go off to school with holes in the bottoms of the only ones I owned. And none of this would have happened if Grandma hadn't been able to reach down into her secret stash and come up with the money for the down payment.

Old Al never pressed her about where that money come from, and she never volunteered the information, but if you just spent some time watching that old lady's habits, it wasn't hard to figure out.

Old Al couldn't read and he couldn't add or subtract, but Grandma'd been to school through the seventh grade, so she handled all the business of the place. When Old Al sold a horse or something, he'd give the money to her, and when he wanted to buy something, he'd ask her for whatever he needed. We're not talking high finance here, because things were so tight for so long that these transactions were really small. But still, Grandma kept a close watch on where the money went and it wasn't easy to pry some out of her if there was another way to get the job done.

Grandma was a saver. She always said, "It ain't what you make, it's what you save," and she'd harp on that and say it so damn many times I got sick of hearing it. It seemed like she was always on the lookout for a chance not to spend money, and it got to be a real pain in the butt. There'd be times when I was a kid in Kila when I'd want a candy bar and I'd go ask her for a nickel.

She'd say, "Go get three eggs and trade 'em to Branch for a candy bar."

So I'd run out to the hen house and get three eggs and trade them at Branch's store for a candy bar. In the end I was taken care of with my candy, and Grandma still had her nickel.

Grandma'd been pulling this kind of stuff all her life. There was the time my Aunt Gladys wanted a permanent for her hair. Gladys was about eighteen at the time, and went to Grandma for some money to get it done.

Grandma said, "Trade 'em a turkey."

Gladys was so mad at her. "Here I was," she said, "with this damn turkey in a gunnysack throwed over my shoulder! I had to walk into town carryin' this son-of-a-bitch of a turkey to trade for a permanent! A live turkey!"

"Well, you got your permanent," Grandma said, "and you was pretty afterwards."

She did the same thing the time I wanted the victrola this old woman in Kila had for sale. It was the old wind-up kind and I really wanted it, so I told Grandma about it.

"Well, I ain't givin' you no money," she said. "Why don't you try to trade for it?"

So I went over and offered this old woman half a dozen chickens and, to my surprise, she said, "Yeah."

So I went home and Grandma said to just go out and catch up six of them fryers. I stuffed them bastards in a sack and carried them over, gave them to the old lady, and got some friends to help me carry my new victrola home.

The nice thing about that victrola was I could play it whenever I wanted, unlike the radio in the living room. Grandma really rode herd on that. It was powered by a six-volt car battery, and when that battery ran down, we'd have to take it into Kalispell and pay to have it recharged. Grandma didn't like to pay for that, so she really restricted our listening. We heard the news every night, and on Saturday she'd let I and Old Al hear two other programs. One was *The Lone Ranger*, which Al liked, although he'd make fun of it.

"Who ever heard of an Indian sayin' 'Get 'em up, Scout?'" he'd laugh.

And then we got to listen to *Happy Cap* at seven. His real

name was Howard something, and during the week he drove the stage between Kalispell and Marion. He'd make the run out in the morning, delivering mail, and on the way back he'd pick up the cans of cream we'd set out by the county road and take them on in to the Glacier Dairy. On his run back a couple of days later, he'd drop off the empty cans.

Anyway, he had this show on KGEZ radio in Kalispell. He'd play guitar and sing and stuff like that for half an hour, and Grandma let us listen to him. One day I was picking up the cream cans and I asked him, "How 'bout singin' a song for me?"

"O.K., I will," said Howard. "You listen Saturday night."

So there I was that Saturday when *Happy Cap* come on, and I heard him say, "I got an old ridin' pard out there at Kila by the name of Monty Hall. I'm gonna dedicate this song to him."

The song he done was "The Old Black Steer in the Draw," and I never have heard it since.

But that was the extent of our radio listening. Grandma'd always say, "Gotta save that battry!" and she'd shut it off.

Grandma rarely bought anyone new clothes. She'd poke through the secondhand stores until she found something that would work, and she also made a lot of clothes. Only problem with that was she was not a seamstress. One sleeve would always be longer than the other and things like that, but she'd just say, "Well, here, just tuck this up like that." No two buttons ever matched. She'd sew a green button on a brown shirt, or a big one next to a little one, didn't matter, you just put a button on and went to school.

So Grandma hated seeing people spend money on unnecessary things, and for me that meant comic books. Gosh, I loved comic books! You could get them for a dime in Branch's Store, and whenever I'd have a dime from some little job I'd done for someone, I'd want to buy a comic book. But Grandma wouldn't let me. So I'd sneak over and buy one anyway, and then I'd crumple up the cover so it'd look used, and when I brought it home I'd tell her I'd borrowed it from Vlasak or one of my other friends.

Speaking about unnecessary things, I often wondered how much she objected to Old Al buying licorice cigarettes for me. They certainly were a waste of money on the one hand. But on the other, they added a whole lot of pleasure to my young life. She never said, because it was something Old Al wanted to do for me. But that was the kind of thing Grandma would frown on.

One time I had a little money and she caught me spending it on something she thought was unnecessary, and that night she wrote in the margin of a page in her Bible, "Monty spent his money foolishly. Now he don't have any. Maybe some day he'll learn that you got to save."

Grandma wasn't only a good saver, she saw opportunities to make money everywhere. Her turkeys were her big enterprise, of course, and they really helped out when she'd unload them every Thanksgiving and Christmas. But she also had her eye out for other chances to make a dollar.

The people who lived on the place before we did had a kind of a junkyard and they left a lot of stuff behind. Old Al gave the biggest pieces of iron and steel machinery to the army, which was looking for scrap iron as it got ready to go to war. But the smaller pieces Grandma gathered up and sold.

And then she went poking around at the sight of the original mill, the one that burned down on the shore of the lake. She'd find a piece of iron half buried, and then she'd get me and her son Leslie, and we'd hitch up the team and go down and help her pull it out. She'd get it all piled up and call the man from the junkyard in Kalispell and he'd come out and pay her so much a ton.

So little by little, by saving and by earning wherever she could, Grandma kept the place afloat. And every now and then, she'd skim some off the top and slip it into that can of talcum powder. That was her private savings account, her measure of security in those insecure times. And nobody even knew it was there until the day Old Al came in and said he was ready to make a move to better ground, but just didn't have the money to pull it off.

He was sixty-eight years old then, past time for new starts for the majority of men, but he seemed to believe he had enough left inside himself for just one more try, to own his own land once again, to know when he lay down weary at the end of the day that he'd spent his time working on a place of his own, that he was his own man once more. If it just weren't for the fact that Willis March wanted four hundred dollars down payment.

It was then that my Grandma, who objected to comic books and wouldn't buy me a candy bar, the lady of the turkeys and the buttons that didn't match, reached down into Budd's trunk and rescued an old man's dreams.

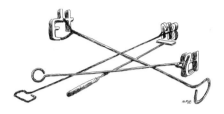

Horse Traders Young . . .

Horse trading was an important part of life in western Montana when I was growing up. I don't know whether horse traders are born with skill or whether you can acquire it. But it took a good eye and a poker face. Often, both sides of the trade thought they'd unloaded a problem on the other guy. Often, both were right. I made my first horse trade when I was nine years old.

I spent a lot of time hanging around the stockyards in Kila on Gypsy, that little half-Shetland pony. We had a rancher friend named Louie O'Connell from over in Niarada who would trail his sheep cross country to the yards. He'd seen me riding around and noticed that I was getting a little big for that pony, and he thought Gypsy would be just about right for his six-year-old grandson. So he proposed a trade.

I wound up swapping him Gypsy for a regular horse, a bay mare Grandma named Dolly. But a key part of the deal was that I would get the foal Gypsy was carrying after it was weaned.

This was an especially important part of the bargain for me, because I'd been on the short end of a deal with Old Al for a couple of years. We'd agreed that he'd breed my Gypsy to one of his stallions for free on the condition that if a stud colt was born, he'd get it. I'd get to keep the fillies. So far, all Gypsy'd had was colts, so all I'd got out of it was the privilege of riding my pony with one of Al's colts by her side.

But now that I'd traded Gypsy away, my deal with Old Al was terminated, and I'd finally get a foal from her. This was fine with Louie O'Connell, so off he went, back to Niarada with a new pony for his grandson.

Gypsy foaled in the spring, and sure enough, it was another stud colt. By fall it was weaned and ready to come home, and I wanted it.

So Old Al told me to go and get it. Keep in mind that I'm just nine years old, and my Grandpa's proposing that I ride twenty-five miles ahorseback, up the old Flathead Mine Road, over the divide in the mountains, down Nine Mile Hill over country I'd never seen before, all the way to Niarada to pick up this colt and lead it home. I'd be gone for at least a couple of days, and there were no phones between us and Louie O'Connell's place, so they'd have no way of knowing whether I'd made it or not, or when to expect me back.

But I wasn't afraid, not one little bit. When Old Al told

you to do something, you just did it. What Grandma thought about this I'll never know, but I suspect they had words about it after I'd left. She packed me a lunch and kissed me good-bye and told me to be a good boy, and off I went.

Actually, it wasn't that big a deal, because I'd be on the county road the whole way, and Al had given me real good directions. He told me where I'd come to Brown's Meadows, and he told me, "You'll get way up on top and there's a big spring right by the side of the road with a sign on it that says 'Welcome Spring.' You eat your lunch there.

"Then you'll drop down the other side," he said, "and when you get down to the bottom you'll come to a ranch. This friend of mine has his house right square in the middle of the road."

I'll never forget how that amused him. And today, if you drive over the Nine Mile Road you'll see the house Walt Jackson now lives in sitting just off the county road.

And then Old Al told me about this point of rocks, which would be Rattlesnake Point. He said just go past there and through a wire gate and after a couple more miles you'll be in Louie's yard.

Sounded simple enough, so off I rode in the warm October morning, thinking about the colt that would soon be mine, and about the big horse ranch I'd have someday. Things went fine until I got above Brown's Meadows.

In those days, everybody turned their stock out. Their

horses ran loose on the range, it was all open range. I topped this knoll and ran smack into this bunch of horses, loose horses, and there was a stud in the bunch—fifteen, twenty mares—and this stud, a-squeelin' and looking at me.

Deep down I knew I was O.K., because I was riding a mare and I remembered Grandpa talking about my Uncle Howard holding a bunch of horses up in Canada with a stud among them. Howard always rode a mare because a stud will leave her alone. If I'd been riding a gelding, I'd of been in big trouble. That stallion would have attacked him, and I mean right now.

What I was really afraid of was my mare breaking loose and running off with the stud and the other horses and leaving me afoot, fifteen miles from home. So there I stood with this stud squealing and stomping and my mare getting prancy, when suddenly I saw the horse with the crimped ears.

I'd never seen a horse with crimped ears before, but I remembered my Grandma singing a song to me about the Strawberry Roan, a horse with "little pin ears that crimp at the tip." This one was black and her ears come up like a horse's ears, but then they curled in and damned near touched. I can remember that today as plain as can be.

Anyway, there I was in a face-off with this squealing stallion, with Grandma's song about the Strawberry Roan going through my head, about to be stranded a long ways from home. So I picked up some rocks and started chucking them at the horses. Off they ran with the stud after them.

Sometime later, I'd gone down the long hill and past Rattlesnake Point, through the wire gate, and a couple of miles further on, sure enough, I wound up in Louie O'Connell's yard, just like Grandpa said I would, and I told Louie I was there to pick up my colt.

Louie O'Connell was a very nice man who loved children although he'd never had any of his own. Mrs. O'Connell had two boys when he married her, and he raised them, and then along came this grandson, and Louie really liked him. This little kid would follow Louie all around the place, and was always with him.

Well, when I pulled into the yard and announced that I'd come for my colt, this kid starts whining about how Gypsy was his pony and how the colt was Gypsy's and how he'd played with it all summer. He kept whining away, "Grandpa, I want that colt." And this put Louie in a real bind.

He'd made a deal with me, man-to-man, so to speak, and I'd ridden a long way to get what was rightly mine. If I'd told him to hand over that colt, he'd of handed me the lead rope, and that would have been that. But then he would of been left with that whiner to deal with. Louie loved this little kid so much, well, to be frank, this kid could of crapped in Louie's face and it would of been fine.

It was then that Louie had an inspiration that saved his reputation with his grandson, improved mine with Old Al, and taught me a lot about horses and horse traders.

"Tell you what," says Louie. "I've got a bunch of horses up in the pasture there. Why don't you go see if there's something you like, and I'll trade you for the colt."

So I rode up the hill through Louie's fields and into his pasture where the horses were, and there was this pretty good-looking black mare with a colt by her. My nine-year-old brain started working and I said to myself, "Hey, I can still make a pretty good deal here because this kid wants my colt real bad."

So I rode back to Louie and told him, "O.K., I'll trade ya for the black mare *and* her colt."

He didn't really want to do it, but he did.

The next day as I was getting ready to head for home, a man named George McCullum (later state senator from Sanders County) drove into the yard with a stock truck. He visited with Louie awhile, and I heard him say he was headed for Kalispell.

"You've got to go through Kila to get to Kalispell, don't you?" I asked.

He allowed as how he did.

"So would you haul these horses and me home on your way?"

He said sure, so we rode back.

I remember when we pulled into the yard at home Old Al came out onto the porch and wanted to know what I had, so

I told him. Grandma told me later he turned to her and said, "By God, that kid might be all right. He leaves with one horse to pick up one, comes back with three, and has 'em hauled home."

Pretty slick, huh? Well, unfortunately, that's not the end of the story.

Grandma named the black mare Niarada because that's where she'd come from. She was a good-looking horse, about fifteen hands, two inches tall, with white hind feet, and a white stripe on her face. She was five years old and hadn't been broke to ride. I knew that, because Louie'd told me. What he hadn't told me was that other men had tried to break her, and failed.

Well, we went through all the proper procedures in the round corral. I got so I could saddle her and drive her with long lines. Then came time for me to get on her. She bucked me off. Every time I got on that horse, she bucked me off, bad.

One day, I figured if I could get her snubbed up to another horse, I could ride her around and she'd get used to having me on her back. So I asked Old Al, "Will ya snub her up?"

"Hell yes," he says, "I'll snub her up."

So he grabbed the lead rope and drew her head right up against his saddle horn.

I stepped on her. He says, "Are ya on?"

I said, "Yeah."

And he just undone the rope and handed it to me.

The son-of-a-bitch bucked me off again.

I picked myself up and said, "I wanted you to lead her around!"

"Oh," he replied, "I thought you was havin' trouble gettin' on!"

Well, I never could ride that horse, and Al suggested I just breed her and turn her out to pasture, which I did.

We turned our horses loose in Dower's Draw, twenty-five or thirty head of mares. We'd turn them out when the grass started coming on, usually about May, and leave them until fall. I got one colt out of Niarada, and a couple of years later she got her final lick in on me.

As I've said, most of this was open range. The law said then (and still does now) that if a automobile driver hits an animal on a road that goes through open range, the driver has to pay for the animal. Road signs clearly indicate where the open range starts. One mile west of Kila, drivers would see a sign that said "Range Stock At Large," and it would be open range all the way to Libby.

From that sign east, toward Kalispell, was the herd district, where you can't let your animals run loose on the highway. If you do, and a car hits one, the animal owner has to pay for the damage to the car.

We had these horses summered up in Dower's Draw, as usual, but for some reason they decided to come out of the hills on their own, early.

I and Al were working around the place that summer day when I was about fourteen when a kid came running over from the post office, where the nearest phone was. He said Deputy Sheriff Walt Manning wanted to talk with Al. Well, of course, Al sent me running back.

Manning was a friend of ours, and also the brand inspector for that district. He said he'd heard that a truck had just hit a horse on the road above our place, and he wanted me to run up and check the brand. The accident had happened within the herd district, so the animal's owner would be responsible for the damages, and Manning wanted to know who to go after.

I went up there, and what do you know? There was Niarada, the black mare I never could ride, deader than hell. I went back down and told Al the news. We were probably looking at several hundred dollars worth of damages due the owner of the truck. I sure as hell didn't have it, and Al didn't either.

"You get back up there," Al said to me, "and cut that brand off of her."

So I went back up, and I took my knife and I cut the hide with the brand on it off. Then I gashed her shoulder like the truck had tore her up hitting her. Then I went back to the post office and called old Walt.

"I don't know who the hell she belongs to," I told him. "I've never seen her before."

. . . Horse Traders Old

My education in horse trading continued the spring after my ride to Niarada. I was ten years old, and the lesson was delivered by two genuine masters of the art, Old Al and a neighbor named George Bruce.

Bruce was a professional horse trader, that's what he did for a living, and he was always after Al to trade with him. He was always coming around asking, "Got anything you want to trade, Al?" Usually Al didn't, but this spring he did.

We'd just brought a bunch of horses in from the winter range, and among them was a good-looking bay gelding, three or four years old, not broke to ride yet, but a really nice-looking saddle horse type. Al noticed he was limping, and when he trotted he held one hind foot off the ground, carried it like a dog with a broken leg. We looked closer at him when he was standing still and could see that the front of that hind foot turned up at a funny angle when it was on the ground. He'd obviously broken something in his ankle or in the foot itself.

That made him useless to us on the ranch. About all we could do with him was lead him over to Bob Denton's mink farm and get maybe ten or fifteen dollars for him as mink food. But Old Al wasn't about to give up on him yet, not with George Bruce the professional horse trader licking his chops every time he came by.

I and Old Al put that bunch of horses in a corral, and not just any corral, either. This particular one hadn't been cleaned yet, and had about a foot of manure and slop accumulated from cows and horses over the winter. It was all melting now, and real soggy, and the horses sank in it real deep. Are you getting the picture?

Old Al told me to saddle up and ride over to George Bruce's place and tell him we'd just brought some horses in and maybe we could make a trade. Bruce came right on over, anxious as always, maybe just a bit more so, and we took him out to the corral.

Old Al led out this bay gelding with the broken foot, nice and slow so he walked normal, and when he stood there his feet were buried in the slop and he looked just dandy. Bruce walked around him and petted him and looked at him standing there in good flesh, a fine young horse with a nice disposition, and he said O.K. He'd take him in trade for a workhorse he had on his place. This was a horse Al had seen before, so he said, O.K., it's a deal, and Bruce went off to get him.

When Bruce came back with the horse, he looked at Grandpa and said, "Al, I think there's one thing I should tell you, because you're gettin' old and I see this kid drivin' the teams.

"The trade is made, but I just want to warn you, don't let this kid drive this horse because he runs away. He runs away bad."

Old Al just said, "Well, it looks like you got me George."

And then he led the bay gelding out onto solid ground where Bruce could plainly see that hind foot turned up. Bruce wasn't a bit happy, but he was honorable. The trade had been made and that was that. If he hadn't been in such a hurry to unload that runaway workhorse, he might have looked the bay over more carefully, but he didn't and now *he'd* get to lead him down to the mink farm.

Grandma named that workhorse George, in honor of his former owner, and we took him to my Uncle Howard's ranch and put him to work with the haying crew.

Uncle Howard teamed him up with a young sorrel mare who was working her first summer, and hitched them to a hay boat. A hay boat is kind of like a big, flat sled without runners, about eight feet wide and sixteen feet long. It slides along the ground on boards that get rubbed slick and smooth as glass, which makes it easier for the horses to pull.

The whole haying operation was done with horses. Horses pulled the mower and they pulled the dump rake, which piled the hay in windrows. Then somebody'd drive the hay boat along and the "pitchers" would fork hay onto it. When it was loaded they'd drive it over to the stack and add that load to the pile.

The result of this labor was piles of hay that sort of looked alike. But since they were all kind of uneven, it was hard to tell just by looking how much hay there actually was in any particular haystack.

This was a pretty big deal, because hay was a major cash crop in Montana in the 1930s and '40s. As the Great Depression began, twenty-six percent of Montana's cropland was devoted to hay, most of it alfalfa and wild grasses, some of it timothy and clover, some of it hay made from grain. The only crop more significant than hay was wheat.

But just how much hay was in that stack out there in Howard's field? Without a sure way to measure it, no seller of hay, like my Uncle Howard, would know what to charge, and no buyer would know what he was getting for his money. Obviously, what everybody needed here was some wisdom from the state capital. And we got it.

In 1935, the Montana State Legislature decided to bring order to all this chaos in Howard's hay field and passed a new law that would answer everybody's questions about haystacks anywhere in the state. Here's what they decided:

For making measurements of hay in stack, the following

is hereby made the legal method of measurement, to-wit:
The width and length of the stack shall be measured, and
the distance from the ground against one side of the stack,
to the ground against the other side of the stack, directly
over and opposite, shall be taken in linear feet and inches,
and then the width shall be subtracted from the measurement
over the stack, as above indicated, the result divided by two,
and the result so obtained multiplied by the width, and the
result thus obtained multiplied by the length, which will
give the number of cubic feet contained in the stack, and
the tonnage shall thereupon be determined by dividing the
total number of cubic feet by the number of cubic feet
allowed under the provisions of this act for a ton.

Or, to put it another way, they said I could ride past a
haystack in Uncle Howard's field and know that its volume
(V) was:

$$V = \frac{O - W}{2} WL$$

This was what they called the Frye Bruhn rule. But it only
worked if the cross sections of the haystacks were rectangles.
If they were squares, they told us the formula would be
different:

$$V = \frac{O + W^2}{4} L$$

In both cases, "O" is the distance over the stack, ground-to-ground, "W" is the width, and "L" is the length.

So, maybe it was possible for a guy to know the amount of hay in a stack in the Flathead Valley on a summer day without lugging the whole pile to a scale.

The bureaucrats at the Department of Agriculture in Washington, D.C. spent an awful lot of time on our haystack problem, too. Their solution was:

$$V = [(0.52xO) - (0.44xW)] WL$$

I am not kidding here. This is all true, and it gets more complicated.

Not to be outdone, the agricultural engineers at the Experiment Station in Bozeman studied the physics of haystacks for twenty years, starting in 1916. They discovered that the average weight of the hay at any given point in a stack could be determined by this formula:

$$W = 2.6 + 0.1D - 0.04X$$

"D" being the depth from the top of the stack to the point, "X" being the distance from the center line.

Nobody expected Uncle Howard, leaning on the top rail of his fence at the end of a hard day, gazing at the fruit of his labor, to work this equation in his head. In fact, they allowed as how the formula might not work all the time in all haystacks. But it did demonstrate for us that the density of hay varied within the stack.

I could of told them that, because a forkful don't lift the same every time when you're loading the sled on a cold winter morning. What I and them scientists had both figured out is that hay settled in some places more than others.

About now your typical farmer in Flathead County, reading all these facts in 1936 in Extension Bulletin No. 327, might be wondering if his tax dollars was being spent sanely. But what we all finally found out was that these studies could translate into dollars for us.

After all their poking into the mysteries of haystacks, the folks at the Bozeman Experiment Station arrived at some interesting conclusions.

Agricultural engineer H. E. Murdock reported the results of measuring 615 haystacks of all kinds, from alfalfa to bluejoint to timothy, from all over Montana—the Judith Basin, the Milk River, the Big Hole, and the Gallatin, Missouri, and Flathead valleys.

He found that the Frye Bruhn formula for calculating the volume of a haystack, the Montana law, was wrong. The hay farmer who faithfully followed that law could be shorting himself by some fifteen percent every time he sold his hay, and we're talking some real dollars in a man's pocket here.

Murdock reported that a better estimate of the volume of stacked hay in ol' Howard's field come from modifying the official formula like this:

$$V = \frac{O - 5/6W}{2} \, WL$$

This new formula gave almost exactly the same result as

the one developed by them bureaucrats at the Department of Agriculture in Washington.

That 1935 Montana law was also real specific about how much hay of different varieties would make up a legal ton: 422 cubic feet of bluejoint after it had settled for thirty days was a legal ton, 512 cubic feet of alfalfa or rough slough grass, and so on.

But ol' Murdock's investigators found that not all haystacks made of the same grass weighed the same. There were wide variations in weight, stack to stack, which again I could have told 'em, having forked down my own share.

In the end, the best advice all these scientists could give us was this:

"A satisfactory mutual agreement should be entered into by the buyer and seller of stacked hay as to the method of arriving at the market value of a given volume."

In other words, dicker over it, which is what we'd been doing all along.

The Montana law specifying how much hay a stack contained was repealed in the late '60s.

But anyway, all these formulas aside, in this the summer of my tenth year, 1941, my job was driving the hay boat pulled by George and the sorrel mare. I was expected to work right alongside the adults and put in a full day. The war was on and help was scarce, and so was money for hired hands, so I pulled a full shift like everyone else.

This particular haying crew included me and Uncle Howard and his wife Hazel, two other men whose names I don't remember, and the wife of one of them. We mowed, raked, and stacked hay on about one hundred acres, working from daylight 'til dark. It was hard work but we ate good, Aunt Hazel quitting work a bit before the rest of us to prepare the meals. And before the day in the fields began, she and Uncle Howard would milk the cows, which is how they were really trying to make a living. Times were really tough, and I remember all the talk around the dinner table being about how short the hay crop was.

Anyhow, I drove George and the sorrel mare as they pulled the hay boat around the fields, and it seemed like George was going to work out fine, despite his reputation for running away, as long as I kept a tight rein on him. My Uncle Howard had given me a stern warning about that before we headed out.

"Now Monty," he'd said, "whatever you do, don't lay these lines down. Under *no circumstances* do you *ever* let go of them lines."

And I didn't. I knew I could handle George as long as I watched him all the time.

It was toward the end of one day and we were loaded up and heading for the stack. There was another hay boat ahead of me, driven by the wife of one of the pitchers, and as she slid along over the mowed field quite a little bit of hay fell off her boat. I pulled up alongside it.

I knew all about George's history of bolting, and I remembered Uncle Howard's admonition about never laying the lines down, but I also remembered all the talk about the short hay crop and the tough times. It was the end of a hard day and the horses were tired. They'd behaved well all day, and I figured it would be O.K. for me to hop off for just a minute to fork this spilled hay onto my boat.

I backed those horses up as close to the front of the boat as I could, and I got off and stood on the lines. Then I started forking this little bit of hay onto my pile, thinking I'm doing a good deed by picking it up for my uncle. I'll never understand how in hell those horses knew I didn't have ahold of them. Somehow, they knew, and they took off, jerking the lines out from under my foot.

I managed to grab ahold of one line and hang on, and now I've got these runaway horses circling around me. They're galloping in a circle with me in the middle, kind of like at a circus, the hay boat swinging wide, hay flying all over the place. Uncle Howard sees this from the stack where he's working, and he hollers at me to turn 'em loose.

So I let 'em go, and off they went through the fields. They went through three wire fences before they got back to the corrals. The boat was tore all to hell, and the harnesses were all tore up. All they had on when they got home was their collars, and the tug lines that used to be attached to the boat.

That ended George's haying career at Uncle Howard's, and back he went to spend the rest of the summer with Old Al.

When summer was over, we turned George and our other horses out on land near Smith Lake. This was an interesting piece of ground. It was really a huge swamp, four or five hundred acres of real bog, so loose and gooey you couldn't walk on it, and a horse sure couldn't. It'd just sink in, and keep on sinking. I once pushed a twelve-foot pole straight down into this boggy ground with one hand. We called the stuff the bog was made of "loon shit."

But in the winter, it was terrific range for horses. It was covered with slough grass, and after an early freeze, slough grass stays green on the stem all winter, so the horses have plenty to eat, and once the bog is frozen solid, they have no trouble walking on it. Except where a muskrat has made a run.

Muskrats lived in the bog, and as they went about their business they made muskrat runs, kind of paths they'd use over and over. These runs through the bog would fill up with water and never freeze really solid because the muskrat kept using them.

Every once in a while, a horse would break through the thin ice into a muskrat run, start sinking into the "loon shit," and he'd be stuck good. Usually, we found them in time, and would pull them out with a rope. But not George.

By the time we found him, only his head was sticking out,

ice solid all around his neck. He must have been there a couple of weeks. George, the runaway workhorse, had froze to death in the icy water of a muskrat run.

A Family Tradition

So as I grew I observed the horse traders in my family enough to pick up on their philosophy and absorb it into my own small brain. It's not that they were crooked, really, but they sure believed in letting the buyer beware, and I picked up on it because they were my heroes.

Take Uncle Howard, for example. God, how I worshipped that man. He and Old Al were two alike, just different in years. It's true, I spent every day trailing along at Al's side. I wanted to please him, and even tried to walk just like him. He was the most important man in my life. But he was getting on. He'd been over sixty when I'd come to live with them, and though he could still cowboy and all that, he was older.

But Howard was a young man, bold and dashing. He'd ride up into our yard smiling and looking fine, nothing heavy on his mind, no task too tough or too dangerous, no horse he wasn't willing to ride. I think every kid picks out someone they want to grow up to be just like, and for me it was my Uncle Howard.

I remember one time him and Aunt Hazel were over in Niarada at Coke Herman's place. There was a man there with one short leg and he wore a real thick sole on his left boot to make him even. He had this great big sorrel gelding standing at the corral there. He stood seventeen hands, and they called him Hightower.

This guy says, "I would give fifty dollars to anybody who could break that horse to ride."

Well, Howard was getting fifteen dollars apiece to break horses back then. He had his saddle in the back of his 1936 Ford, so he just says, "Where is he?"

This son-of-a-bitch was dirty and he was mean and he was just a bad horse. Howard saddled him and got on him and this horse bucked like hell. But he didn't buck him off, and Howard finally got him to running. He run him around and around and around that corral, and then he yelled at Coke to open the gate, and out they went. Howard headed him straight toward the Nine Mile Hill out of Niarada on the run.

What he was doing was heading for Old Al's place over the same route I'd taken to pick up my colt from Louie O'Connell, only in reverse. When Howard got to the start of the Nine Mile Hill, he broke the horse back to a trot, and he trotted that son-of-a-bitch all the way back to Old Al's. When he pulled into our place, that horse was ringing wet, but he wasn't wanting to buck, I'll guarantee you that.

He turned out to be one hell of a good horse, but it took miles. I was over to Howard's the day the man came and picked him up. It scared Aunt Hazel so bad, because when he got on him he had to work that foot with the thick sole into the stirrup to step up on him, and he was stuck there for sure. But, boy, he rode him around there, and he was a-reining good, and this guy was so tickled with him.

That fifty dollar breaking fee made a payment on Howard's ranch that fall.

So this was my idol. I wanted to be just like him, so I learned his lessons well. Like the one about trading knives, sight unseen.

I was about eight that day when he rode up and said, "Say, Monty, you wanna trade knives?" And he stuck out his fist with a knife hidden in it.

Well, hell, I had a knife. Aunt Hazel had just given me a pair of high-topped boots, the lace-up kind—so tall Old Al had said he'd have to wake me up a half hour early for school just so I could lace 'em up. There was a sheath at the top of one of them boots with a silver-colored knife with three blades in it. So I took it out and hid it in my fist and poked it out at Uncle Howard.

Then we both opened our hands. He walked off laughing with my silver knife and I was standing there looking at one with one broken blade.

Next time he come into the yard, I run up and said, "Hey, Uncle Howard. You wanna trade knives?"

"Sure," he says, and he held out his fist. I held out mine, too. Hidden in my little paw was the broken-bladed knife he'd stuck me with last time.

But he got me again with one that was worse.

Uncle Howard never made any big lesson about life out of this. In fact, he never said nothing, just walked off laughing every time he left me with a worse knife. But you didn't have to have much brain cavity to get the point. Like the day he wanted me to help him stretch his new rope.

He'd said, "This is a brand new rope, Monty, and I want to stretch it. Hang onto it."

Well, I was little and I hung onto it and pulled, him on the other end. He says, "Pull harder!"

So I dug in and pulled for all I was worth, leaning back on my heels, and he turned it loose. Down I went. And off he went, laughing.

But that only happened once. After that, I stuck one foot out behind me when I stretched his rope.

With every experience, I was learning about how to get along in those times. Like I said, neither Grandpa or Uncle Howard ever sat me down and explained things to me, or tried to make sure I got a particular point. Maybe it was because Old Al never had a father of his own who explained things to him, and they say we learn how to be parents by watching our own. Whatever, they just let me hang around them all the time, and figured I'd catch on. Like the time I was about six and they sold Comanche to old Willis March.

Willis March was a good man with a super education, and an honest man, well liked. Only thing was, Old Al said, when it came to livestock the only thing Willis lacked was common sense.

Willis had a real thing about a horse's name. He once named a horse Morning Glory just so he could go out to the corral first thing in the day and say, "Good morning, Glory!" And he'd always wanted a horse named Comanche.

Old Al had a nice bay gelding he'd raised named Comanche, and Willis wanted to buy it. He owned a dude ranch with lots of horses on it, and I guess it never occurred to him to rename one of them Comanche. I mean, a horse ain't like a dog, where his name means something to him.

But Willis had to have a horse that had been named Comanche from the start, so Old Al sold him one, and Willis took him back to the dude ranch. He had a lot of range leased in the Truman Creek area about five miles from our place, and in the spring of the year he turned his horses loose until the dudes arrived in the summer. Well, as soon as he turned Comanche loose, the horse came home to our place, as a horse will.

That spring, Boots Coombs was wanting to buy some horses for the border patrol, so Howard and Old Al got some in and were pulling their tails and making them look good for the sale. Comanche was tied up along with the rest.

I was just a little guy, but I'd grown up with that horse, and I'd seen him sold to Willis March. So I shouted out to Old Al, "Hey, that's Comanche!"

Old Al said, "Hell, what do you know? That ain't Comanche." And he hung some other name on the horse.

"Yes it is, too!" I said. "That's Comanche!"

Old Al and Howard went into a huddle, and I could hear 'em referring to "that kid." I was allowed to stay under the condition that I kept my mouth quiet during the sale, and when it was over they'd sold Comanche for a second time, and Boots Coombs took him off to work for the border patrol. Willis March never missed him, or if he did he never said nothing about it. Old Al always maintained that Willis didn't know what he owned or didn't own.

The lesson I learned there was to just keep my mouth shut about some things and everything'd be O.K. Like when we killed deer out of season. I came to know you just didn't say nothing about it to nobody, just did it and ate 'em, burned the hide, and that was that.

What we're talking about here is getting by during the years of the Depression, and Old Al got by. Like the winter he had half a dozen real good horses and not enough hay to feed them. He knew Willis had plenty of hay for his dude string, so Al and me took tweezers and plucked the long winter hair off our horses rumps in the shape of Willis' brand.

Al turned them out in Willis' lane and called him up and told him some of his stock had got loose. Willis retrieved them and fed them all winter, and when he turned them out with the rest in the spring, they came home. All that long winter hair eventually shed off, and with it the evidence of our "branding" job.

And still, Old Al never commented on these doings. He just assumed I was getting the point by being with him and with Howard and watching, and on my part, I just assumed that this was the way to do business.

There was only one time I remember that Old Al walked me through a deal. I was fifteen and this girl my age brought a colt to me and asked if I'd break it for fifteen dollars. I said, "You bet!" and started to work with the horse.

This was one of them horses that just wants to learn. He was so fine, the first time I put the saddle on him, he didn't buck, he laid down. Gosh, he was a good bastard, and I really liked him, and Old Al liked him really well, too, and the more I rode him, the better he got. And the more I wanted him.

One day when I was working with him, Al asked me, "What are they gonna do with him?"

I said, "They're gonna sell him."

"How much they want?" he asked.

I told him, "A hundred and a half." And then I said, "I sure would like to have him."

So he told me what to do.

I went down to this girl's place and got my face looking as long as it could, and I asked her, "Did that horse come home?"

This girl had a real mouthy mother, and right away she just flew apart. "Whadda ya mean, 'Did that horse come home?'!?"

I said, "He got away from me."

This mother started raising all kinds of hell. So, I said, "Well, I'll tell you what I'll do. I'll give you fifty dollars and just take my chances on finding him."

Boy, she stuck her hand right out. A minute later, they had fifty dollars and I had a good horse. When I got home, my Grandpa was waiting for me.

"You get him?" he asked.

"Yeah," I answered.

"Then," said Old Al, "you handled it good."

The Herdsman

I was over at the Kila Post Office one day in the spring when I was eleven and I heard some men talking about how there was going to be a new program to kill these gophers that were all over the country. They were going to use some kind of poison and needed to hire some people with horses to work all summer long.

The man doing the talking was Albert Sales from over in Thompson River, and I got the idea by listening that he was the man you had to see about one of those jobs.

I ran right home to check it out with Old Al, and he said fine, I could do it if I wanted to. Sales told me the man I should talk to was Walter Rau. Well, hell, this thing started looking like it was in the bag. Walter was the caretaker at the county fairgrounds and I'd known him since I was a little kid. Sure enough, he gave me a job riding on the new gopher crew he was putting together, and the job would last all summer.

This was the best deal ever. I'd get paid four dollars a day
—*four dollars*—at age eleven, and me used to working at home
for nothing. I had to supply my own horse, but that was sure
no problem 'cause I had a mare called Goldie to ride. I'd have
to live up at Walter's place in Kalispell during the week, but
that was no problem either. They'd take seventy-five cents a
day out of my pay to feed me, and seventy-five cents a day to
board my horse, put her up and give her hay. If I wanted to
feed her grain, I'd have to bring that from home. I'd live in a
tent in Walter's yard with another kid, and I'd get to go home
on weekends. We wouldn't get our pay during the summer.
That money would just keep accumulating and I'd get it when
the job was done.

There were four of us on the crew plus Walter, who was
the foreman, me and this other kid who's name I can't
remember, and two men. Every day we'd saddle up and get
two big sacks of poison oats from Walter. They'd hang from
the saddle horn, one down each side of the horse's shoulders,
and off we'd go, loaded for gopher.

We'd stop at every ranch and farm in Walter's district and
proceed out into the fields where the gophers were tearing
things up. The farmers generally didn't want us spreading
the poison too near the yard, but out in the fields was fine.
We'd ride along in a line with Walter directing us, kind of
weaving through the field, and every time we'd come to a
gopher hole we'd sprinkle some poison oats around it.

What you'd do is take just about what you could hold in your thumb and two fingers and drop it around the entrance to the hole. The gopher would eat it and eventually crawl back into his hole to die. That way, generally, nothing else'd eat *him* and die in turn. At noontime, we'd stop for lunch there in the field. We wore no gloves, never washed our hands before eating, and I can still remember the taste of that poison on my fingers as I ate my sandwiches.

It seemed like there were gopher holes everywhere, and we sure had plenty of customers. It was good work for an eleven-year-old kid, ahorseback all day long, sleeping in a tent, all that money piling up.

The only negative thing about it was that Walter Rau had this crummy little daughter named Isabel. She was a couple of years younger than me, and I mean this was really a rotten little kid. While we were out bumping off gophers all day, she was back at the place stuffing leaves and grass and other junk in my sleeping bag. This got very tiresome. I never could make her quit it, and forty-six years later, can you believe it, she told me she did it because she had a crush on me. I wonder if she still does?

Anyway, that summer eventually came to an end and I went to the county agent's office to get my pay, minus what they took out for board for me and my horse. It came to one hundred and thirteen dollars. They gave it to me in cash, one big wad that I stuffed down in the pocket of my jeans, and I headed straight for the Woolworth store in Kalispell.

Remember those rows of glass jars with different kinds of candy in them? I'd never had any money to get any of that candy, but I was sure about to make up for lost time now. I was standing there looking over the prospects when my Aunt Hazel, Howard's wife, come along and asked me what I was doing.

"Look at this, Aunt Hazel!" I said, and dragged out my wad of money. "I just got paid!"

Aunt Hazel took that money and counted it, and then she gave me back three dollars of it and kept the rest. She told me she'd give it to Grandma to keep for me. Well, what the hell, I still had three dollars, more than I'd ever had in that store before, and since most of the candy in those jars was a penny apiece, I could stretch it pretty far. And I did, too. I walked out of there with a big sack of candy and started hitchhiking for home. A man named Ed Conrad came along and picked me up and drove me back to Kila, me eating candy all the way.

That fall, Slim Bloomer had an auction sale up at his place on Truman Creek and I rode up to see it. They were auctioning off some cattle born that year that now weighed maybe four hundred pounds. Old Gilford Marvin was standing there, and I asked him how to bid, and he told me. So I got to bidding on these calves. I wound up buying three of them, two heifers and a steer. They cost me fifteen dollars each.

After the sale there was some other kids there, and I was goofing off with them when ol' Slim come over.

"Monty," he said, "you bought them calves."

I said "Yeah?"

"Well," he said, "you gotta pay for 'em. You can't come to an auction and not pay for 'em."

"I ain't got no money."

"What the hell you mean, you ain't got no money?"

"Well," I said, "I got some, but it's at home. You'll have to go down and get the money from Old Al."

Then I thought about that for a minute and said, "You gonna do it?"

He says, "Yeah."

So I says, "How about haulin' my calves home when you go?"

Later Slim told Old Al, "Goddamn that kid, he comes to an auction with no money, then I gotta haul his calves home to get paid." But he was laughing when he said it. And that was how the money I'd earned killing gophers got me started in the cattle business. I was eleven years old and owner of three calves. I traded the steer to Uncle Howard for a black workhorse, and I kept them heifers to start my herd. When they were ready, I was gonna breed 'em to one of Old Al's bulls.

It's interesting that this desire to get something going was so strong in me at that age. But somehow I knew I had to have animals, had to breed them, had to get a herd going, had to watch it increase. This was just the thing to do, and I'd always felt that way. I was compelled along this path for as long as I can remember, moved to do this thing for reasons I never understood or questioned.

When I was little, about seven, I had a whole bunch of rabbits and was breeding the does to get more. I kept them in hutches and moved them under a flat-roofed shed in the winter. I'd cut grass for them, and at night I'd sneak over to Burlingham's alfalfa field and steal a sackful for my rabbits. I was on my way to becoming a real successful rabbit breeder. I didn't do anything with them, didn't sell them or eat them, just had a lot of them and wanted a lot more.

Old Al hated them bastards. He wouldn't have ate one anyhow, because him and Grandma were always talking about the jackrabbits in Idaho that got sick and got big sores on them. These rabbits of mine didn't contribute a damn thing to the place. They just took up space and food, and Al didn't have any use for them.

But for me, it was sure evidence that I could be a rancher, and I intended to prove it in a really big way. Then one day when my herd of rabbits numbered about twenty, something strange started happening.

I'd breed the does and watch for signs that they were getting ready to give birth. When they made their nest, I knew the time was right. I'd wake up early the next morning, and go running like a son-of-a-bitch out to the hutches to see the babies. And they'd all be dead. Every one of the baby rabbits would be dead. They'd be scattered all over the cage, no hair on them, not snuggled up in the nest nice and warm like they were supposed to be to stay alive. And this happened every single time I'd breed one of my does.

Well, one day I decided I'd had enough of rabbit ranching, and went to Old Al and told him I was going to make a trade for the whole batch of them with my friend Gene Everts.

Old Al said, "Good!"

So I and Gene got a bunch of boxes and put all these rabbits in and hauled them off to Gene's house. I came back that evening leading two little brown goats.

If there was one thing Old Al *really* hated, it was a goat. We had no goats on the place. I mean he had *no* use for the "stinkin' sons-of-bitches." But here I come anyway, prouder than can be, leading the products of my rabbit trade into the barnyard. I put them in a big box stall in the back of the barn and fixed them up with hay and water and went in to bed.

Next morning I got up early and went tearing out to the barn, and there were both my new goats, dead as can be, blood running out of their nostrils. I went running into the house, crying to my Grandpa.

Old Al put his coffee cup down, looked at me and exclaimed, "Why, God Almighty! The only thing I can think of, son, is that they *froze to death!*"

Well, I was about eight years old then, and I believed him. I guess it wasn't until I was twenty and Al was gone that it dawned on me that something was wrong with that explanation. Why, shit, you just can't kill a goat, hardly, and who ever heard of one of them sons-of-bitches freezing to death? In a *barn?* And then I began to wonder about all them dead baby rabbits. And about all those puppies I had that run away.

When I was a little kid, I was always bringing home puppies. Somebody'd have a litter, and I'd ask for one and come home dragging it behind me. They'd all disappear within a day or two, and Al would tell me they'd run away.

I finally figured out that Old Al was behind these strange events. He always got up at four in the morning, and I know now it must have been him that went out early and uncovered the baby rabbits and scattered them about so they'd die, and maybe squeezed their little heads to make sure. And I'm certain he helped my goats "freeze to death." I don't know exactly what happened to them puppies, but he was in on it.

It's not that my Grandpa was mean. And he would certainly understand the part of my nature that made me want to be surrounded by animals and watch them multiply.

But he had his limits.

Fox

The second summer of the gopher wars, I rode for my Uncle Howard on a poisoning team that included my friend Dick Urquart and a fifteen-year-old girl whose name I won't mention because she helped me lose my virginity in Howard's hayloft and she still lives around here.

At twelve, I was a cattle owner, had money in the bank, a good job lined up for the summer, and I was riding about as high as a Montana boy could get in those times. Then, suddenly, it appeared as if it might all come undone when my horse Goldie got a sore back.

Those sacks of poison oats that hung from the saddle horn were heavy, and you had to always try to keep them in balance so the saddle wouldn't shift from one side to the other. I was careful to take my three fingers of oats from one side first, then the other, to keep the weight about equal as the sacks emptied, but it was real hard, and there was a lot of shifting from side to side anyway. That saddle rubbed away on old Goldie's back, and it got so bad I couldn't ride her. No horse, no job.

So, I went to see Old Al. He was out by the barn working, and I noticed for the hundredth time the beautiful sorrel gelding in the corral nearby, just looked at him in passing, thinking what a fine animal he was. It was Fox, and he belonged to my Aunt Gladys, who was away in the shipyards of Portland working as a riveter. Fox was some special horse, so special that the only people who had ever ridden him were Aunt Gladys and Old Al himself. I can see his color in my mind today—red as a sorrel could be and not one white hair on him.

Well, I laid my horse troubles on Old Al, who listened while he kept on working, and when I was done he just said, "Ride Fox."

I was floored. Nobody rode Fox except them two. This was an amazing offer and for a minute I didn't believe I'd heard him right. Then he looked at me and said, "But don't run him. I just put new shoes on him, and the front ones don't fit just right. He'll be fine if you go slow, but *don't run that horse.*"

I assured him that I understood, and I did. Old Al was getting along in years and probably couldn't do the shoeing job he could when he was younger. But my young world was back together again, and not only that, I'd get to ride the most handsome horse on the place, on the gopher team, maybe in all of Flathead County.

All this gopher business had started a couple of years earlier when Leonard Eliason, the Agricultural Extension Agent for Flathead County, called a bunch of farmers together for an important meeting. The subject was how to get rid of this small mammal the locals called "the gopher."

Actually, these little creatures weren't gophers. They were Columbian ground squirrels. Whatever, they were a major pain in the butt for the farmers and ranchers of the Flathead Valley, because the little bastards would dig a horrendous complex of holes and tunnels in a man's fields, and then eat his crops.

It was not a new problem in the West. Ground squirrels had harassed farmers way back in the early 1800s in California, where the folks around the mission at Santa Barbara banded together in the first community campaign to kill the little rodents. They used the poison strychnine. You can learn all this from a 1937 bulletin from the Montana Extension Service, called "Control of Rodent Pests in Montana." It starts off with the following dramatic statement:

"The control of crop-destroying rodents has been one of major concern to the western farmer ever since the first prairie sod was turned under to make way for cultivated crops, and livestock replaced the herds of buffalo, elk and deer."

Well, there sure was no Buffalo Bill of the gopher, so it

was up to Extension Agent Eliason to deal with the problem in Flathead County in 1940. This was a particularly good year for the little pests, and it was an unusually dry year, so the gophers moved into the cropland early.

So there they were, thousands of Columbian ground squirrels, digging and chomping away at the rich cropland of Flathead County when Agent Eliason got his group of farmers together to "secure their cooperation and the cooperation of the county commissioners in setting up an organized program for 1941."

Ol' Eliason convinced 'em. Everyone at that meeting agreed that it was time to solve the gopher problem. The county commissioners agreed to pay for part of the deal, and put a small tax on agricultural land to pay some of the first-year costs. And the Fish and Wildlife Service said they'd help pay the wages of a crew that would prove that you could eliminate the gopher menace if you went about it right.

The next spring they began. They selected portions of the western part of Flathead County to prove their point, parts of the country around Pleasant Valley, Lost Prairie, and Thompson River, where the gopher problem was getting out of hand. The ranchers would pay for the oats, which would be laced with strychnine.

Some things have been around for an awful long time, and the poison strychnine is one of them. That extension bulletin in 1937 said that:

Strychnine has been found to be the most satisfactory toxic agent for controlling most field rodents. It is constant in its action, there is an adequate supply always available, and when used in the proportions and exposed according to the methods recommended, it is practically harmless to the gallinaceous group of birds—quail, pheasants, mountain and sage grouse.

So in the middle of May in 1941, this crew of four men on horseback and their foreman set out to prove that you could do a real job on the gopher if you put your mind to it. Hanging from each side of their saddles ahead of their legs were sacks of oats, doctored with strychnine. They spread out in a line across a field and scattered the bait near every gopher hole they found.

Elsewhere in the county, individual ranchers were also scattering poison bait around the ground as they had for many years. In fact, county extension records show that 137,484 pounds—some sixty-nine tons—of strychnine-laced oats had been spread over Flathead County since 1918. The farmers also attacked the pests with cyanogas. They could purchase the oat bait, the gas, and the strychnine from the county at cost.

This sounds like a really big effort, but the poisoning was all voluntary, and it was haphazard. One farmer might eliminate the gophers from his field, only to have a new bunch move in from next door. What made this 1941 deal different was organization. The Columbian ground squirrel was about to meet up with the scientific method.

The ranchers all thought them gophers would be real hungry when they woke up from hibernation, so they spread poison oats around as soon as the snow disappeared. The results were spotty, and people were losing confidence in strychnine. Extension Agent Eliason set out to restore it.

He knew from scientific studies that real early spring was too early to poison gophers effectively. So he sent a special newsletter to every farmer in Flathead County. And he used the radio and news releases to spread the word: "Early poisoning is not nearly as effective as that done from the time the first young appear until mid-July for this area."

At the end of 1941, Eliason reported to his superiors in Helena that, "A great deal of good was accomplished by this educational program; farmers, instead of blaming the bait for not making good kills, as they had in the past, used more bait than ever before with much better satisfaction."

And that sure was true. In 1940, farmers and ranchers in Flathead County had spread 6,750 pounds of poison oats across their fields. In 1941, the year of the media blitz, the amount jumped to 20,500 pounds. The demonstration project alone laid out about 8,000 pounds, and reported a kill rate of ninety percent.

In July, Eliason took the Flathead County Commissioners out to the test area to show them what organized gopher control could do. The county fathers were so impressed they allocated $5,000 to hire more crews and buy bait to continue the program the following year.

In 1942, five crews assaulted the gopher in Flathead County. In addition, some members of the Kalispell Saddle Club gave up several evenings and weekends for the cause. That year, the paid executioners, volunteers, and individual ranchers dumped 32,000 pounds of strychnine-laced oats on the ground.

The program continued like this for the next several years, and it seemed to be working. The only unhappy note filed by Eliason was in his annual report for 1944, a year when many able-bodied men from Flathead County were overseas dealing with a more serious pest.

He noted:

There was some difficulty in getting crewmen who would do satisfactory work. The shortage of experienced adult workers forced us to use a majority of youths on our crews. One crew consisted largely of rural girls, who did a much more satisfactory job than some of the boys of the same age.

One of the "boys of the same age" was me.

Well, no matter what Agent Eliason thought, me and Fox were working out just great on our gopher team, until one Saturday in the middle of the summer when I and Dick

Urquart decided to go to Kalispell to see a picture show.

We were riding home toward Kila after a week's work that Saturday when we made those plans to go to the movies. We had just reached a stretch of the dirt road that led down a bit, then started climbing again up a pretty steep hill. In the little swale at the bottom was this mud puddle. Dick said he'd race me to the top on the other side and the loser would buy the show tickets. This was a great deal, because I knew Fox could beat his horse, so off we went, flying down the hill.

I don't know whether it was the puddle Fox tried to avoid, or them long front shoes, or what it was, but just as we hit the bottom of that little swale, down he went, and I mean hard, spilling both of us all over that country road, just skidding through the mud. I was a real mess, all skinned up and bruised and bloody, but I was in better shape than Fox.

His shoulder was broken. He just lay there in that muddy swale all busted up, and I got that horrible sick feeling inside of me, the one that comes when you know what you'd do different in life if you just had a chance to do things over again. But sometimes there is no second chance, and in a flash you've screwed it up bad, real bad, and there's no explaining it, or justifying it, no apology that will ever make up for it, no way to ever make it right again. Or so it seems. It's a real helpless feeling, and I was lost and scared and twelve years old, standing in the sunlight of a lovely Montana summer day, shocked, my promise to my Grandpa about not running Fox filling my brain. I had no idea in the world what to do.

Eventually, I ran back to Uncle Howard's place and told him what had happened. He was furious, and stormed off to tell Old Al. I hid. Sometime later, Al came and got me. When we got home, he didn't say one word to me, not one thing about how stupid I was, or how irresponsible, nothing. In fact, he didn't say a thing about Fox until a couple of days later, when out of the blue he says, "You know, Monty, you're going to have to pay for that horse."

The relief and gratitude that rushed though me were unbelievable. You bet I'd pay for that horse, gladly. Turned out Old Al's price tag was two hundred dollars, real hefty for a saddle horse in those days, but considering the alternatives for me, it was just fine. It took all my gopher money from that summer, and all of what I'd saved from the last, and I had to cash in every War Bond my mother had sent me, but I paid Aunt Gladys back. Aunt Gladys, who was, happily, still in Portland playing "Rosie the Riveter."

I finished out the summer on Goldie, whose back had healed up by then, and when the job was done Uncle Howard told me not to bother applying for work with him the next year. I guess he never forgave me for what I'd done to Fox.

Later on, Grandma told me what had happened when Uncle Howard reported the disaster to Old Al. Howard was sputtering and fuming through the tale, madder than hell, while Old Al just listened. At the end of it, Howard said, all agitated, "Well, what do you want to do about the horse?"

"Why, shoot the son-of-a-bitch," Al replied.

"And what about that kid!?!" Howard shouted.

"Hell," said my Grandpa, "I can raise a new horse in three years. It takes twenty-one years to raise a man."

The Long View

The winter after Fox died was a long one for me. All my money was gone, and a lot of my self-respect. But spring always comes, and for me this spring came along with a big surprise.

In March, I and Old Al brought in the horses from the range around Smith Lake. We had to get them in before that loon shit softened up and them horses started sinking in. We were going to separate the mares in foal from the rest, and keep them with us at the ranch until they'd had their colts. The rest we'd turn out up in the Dower's Draw country, where the south-facing hills were already bare of snow and the bunch grass was coming on.

But first Old Al wanted to treat them for wood ticks. That Dower's Draw country was really bad for wood ticks, and Al always said that one tick could kill a yearling if it got up between his ears or on his head or anywhere on the neck and started in on them nerves. The ticks themselves wouldn't kill them, but they'd get them down on the ground. I've never seen an older horse down with ticks, but they'd get a colt for sure.

Old Al had a remedy for this. In the spring he'd go to a service station and get a couple of five-gallon cans full of old oil. He had him an old mop, and he'd dip it in and slop it on their heads and down their backs, and rub it in their heads real good. That kept the ticks off the important parts.

Had to be old oil, though. I remember one time I was turning some horse out and I found some new oil and spread it on. Every damn bit of his hair come off. It grew back in sixty days, but Old Al said, "You damn fool, don't do that. You gotta use used oil."

So we spread on that old black shit. I never understood why there was a difference, and if Al did he didn't share it with me. I never saw anyone else use oil for ticks, but we did.

Anyway, we were separating these horses and sorting them out when he roped a real pretty two-year-old chestnut filly whose mother was Charlemagne, a mare he'd got from Willis March. He got the rope around this filly's neck and leaned on it just a little. She jumped back and tossed her head, lookin' good, you know.

"God," he says, "she's nice, ain't she?"

I says, "Yeah, she really is."

He just handed me the rope and says, "You can have her."

Then he walked away, and told me over his shoulder to put a halter on her because he wanted his rope back.

He never told me why I was getting her. He never come to me and said, "Well, you had to pay for Fox, and I feel bad for you." None of this kind of stuff. He just said, "You can have her."

Grandma, of course, she talked about it. Grandma would go into detail. She told me, "Son, he's givin' you that horse because he figures you learned your lesson, and all your money's gone." But the old man never said nothing about it.

So I was able to start the third summer of the gopher wars with the Fox incident really behind me. I was a new man with a clean slate, a thirteen-year-old cattle owner and horse owner, broke for money but with two summers' experience killing gophers under my belt, and ready to be a top hand on anybody's crew.

Except Uncle Howard's. You'll remember he told me not to bother coming back after last summer. I think he told Grandma I was piss-poor help or something. But it wasn't that, because I'd done a good job, and I don't think it was over Fox, either. I think Uncle Howard was jealous of all the attention I was getting from his parents, particularly his father, Old Al. It's not that Old Al liked me any better. It was just that he had more time to spend with me than he'd had with his own children, now that things had settled down in his own life a bit.

Whatever, I heard about a preacher named Fred Harvey in the Stillwater country northwest of Kalispell who was putting together a gopher crew and I went to see him, since Uncle Howard wouldn't have me. This preacher hired me onto a crew that was all kids, me and his sons Bob and Mick and a couple other boys. That Fred Harvey was the only minister I ever met who I thought was honest.

My churchgoing was a little spotty when I was growing up. Old Al never went. He told me I should live by the Ten Commandments and then left it to Grandma to explain them to me. Grandma made me go to Sunday school, and she talked to me about preaching, and read to me from the Bible, much of which I didn't understand. I had to go to Sunday school at least until I was too big for her to force me, and right after regular school let out for the summer, there was about ten days of Bible school there in Kila, and she made me go to that.

The thing a lot of kids hate about Sunday school is having to get up early to go to it. That part wasn't a problem for me because I was usually up early on Sundays anyway. Old Al got up at four A.M. year-round, and he'd shake me awake before dawn, saying, "I think it's time you got goin', son."

There was a community hall in Kila, you see, where they'd have a Saturday night dance at least a couple times a month, and I'd get up early the morning after to collect the empty beer bottles from the parking lot. I'd get up before dawn and saddle my pony Gypsy and hang a couple of sacks off the saddle horn and off I'd go. No other kid in town was up that early, so I made out real good, selling beer bottles back to the store for a penny apiece. On a good Sunday morning, I could collect a hundred.

But old Fred Harvey was a special kind of preacher. He's the only man I ever met who called himself a pastor who I felt believed in what he was telling you. Seems like all the others want is your dollar. And they've gotta have a church that's a four-million-dollar son-of-a-bitch to preach in, you know. Like these TV preachers, *them* counterfeit bastards, the money they're pulling in. Old Fred would never do anything like that.

One thing I liked about old Fred was he never tried to convert you. I'd cuss in front of him, and he'd never say, "Well, Monty, don't use that kind of language." And if you asked him anything, he'd explain it to you.

One day, I asked him, "Why does God let little kids die?" I couldn't understand that. There was this little girl that died that summer, and I asked him how come God took her.

He told me God needed a little angel by his side. That pacified me. I don't think Fred knew why He done it, but I was satisfied with what he told me.

Anyway, at the end of every day of gopher killing, we'd ride back to Fred's farmhouse, and Mrs. Harvey would have a huge dinner ready for us, lots of vegetables from her garden and beef or chicken. Fred was such a kind soul he'd let all of us kids wash first. Mrs. Harvey'd set out a bucket of hot water and a washbasin on the porch along with a towel, and we'd clean up and comb our hair and then sit at the table, waiting.

And waiting. We'd have to wait for everyone to get done washing out on the porch, and then wait for him, and then he'd say grace, while all this food sat there on the table in front of me, a thirteen-year-old kid so damn hungry. We went through this ritual every night, and the memory of it still annoys me.

The Harveys were some nice family, and Fred worked like a slave for them. His son Bob still ranches northwest of Kalispell, Mike is a teacher down around Bozeman, and Torrance is a preacher like his dad.

One thing Grandma told me at the start of the summer was to be sure to get a recommendation from Fred when the work was over. She reminded me about it every time I saw her, just about, so I asked Fred to do it and he wrote up something real nice. He said, "Monty has worked for me all summer. I don't know if I'm going to have a gopher crew next summer, but if I do I'd like Monty to be on it."

First opportunity she had, Grandma showed that recommendation to Howard. I don't quite know what that was all about, but she made sure Howard saw it.

That fall, two brothers who owned the Sun Valley Ranch eight miles west of Kila were auctioning off everything so they could move to Whitefish. I had money again, so I figured it was time to spend some of it to build up my herd. I bought five heifers, and then I saw this red davenport they were trying to get rid of, too, so I bought it for Grandma, the one in our parlor being all ratty.

We hauled it home in a pickup that belonged to my pal Hank Vlasak's father. Hank was my age and didn't have a driver's license, either, and his dad wouldn't have let him take the truck nohow, so we hot-wired it. Grandma was sure pleased with that davenport.

She was pleased, too, with my progress as a cattle owner. Grandma wanted me to do well in life, and she enjoyed being proud of me. I was making a real good start for a kid, and she wanted me to keep at it. If I kept adding to my herd every summer, I'd have quite a number of cows by the time I was ready to go off on my own. "You've got the cattle now, Monty," she'd say. "When you're ready to go, all's you'll need is the land."

And the herd did get larger, too. For the next couple of years I bought more heifers every fall, and the ones I already had calved. It was really working for me, the herdsman who started with those rabbits, and Grandma's pride kept growing until one day in June when I was fifteen and I saw Ed Fine putting oil in his '36 Chevy four-door at Branch's store in Kila.

Something in my brain snapped, and I knew I had to have

a car. I'm not sure why that powerful notion took ahold of
me, but it did. I guess every kid goes through it, that stage
when suddenly you just don't give a damn about what used
to be so important. All I knew was it was time for me to get
out and look at something besides a cow, and I wanted to get
some girls, and this car was going to be a major part of my
new deal. None of my friends had cars, but that didn't matter.

Fine said he'd sell it to me for $195. A fifteen-year-old
could get a driver's license back then by just going down to
the courthouse and paying seventy-five cents. No test, no
questions. All I had to do was sell my cattle for the money for
the car. I knew a man named Bullshit Kelly in Kalispell who
would buy them cows, so I was all set for my new life.

When I made the big announcement at home, Grandma
threw a fit. I mean she was really mad. She sat me down and
talked pretty damn tough to me.

"You're *not* gonna do this," she said. "You wait 'til your
Grandfather gets here. You're gonna see whether you're gonna
sell them cattle or not.

"I can stop this," she said. "You're under age. I'll have him
arrested if he buys them cattle."

Well, I was mad and disgusted, but I didn't dare talk back
to her. I knew better than that. She'd of slapped the hell out
of me, and then I'd of had Old Al to put up with if I ever said
anything bad to her.

That night at the supper table she brought it up, and I

told Old Al what I wanted to do. Grandma said, "You're *not,*" and she started going on and on and on about it.

Old Al held out his hand and gave several little downward motions with it to mark his words and said, "Whoa, whoa, whoa, just a minute."

When she'd stopped he said, "Well, you might as well let him sell 'em and learn his lesson now while we're still here to kind of look after him a little. He's gotta learn—and he might as well do it while he's young—what a damn fool he is."

So the next week I gathered them sons-of-bitches up off the open range. Bullshit Kelly had him fifteen new cows and I had me a car.

I had a great time for the next three months, and I had plenty of girls, some of them on the back seat, and then the damn thing broke down. You couldn't steer it. We drug it home with a truck. I told Old Al, "You know, it wouldn't take much to fix it."

"Then you better get started," he said, "'cause I ain't givin' you any money."

Well, there that car sat. Grandma never said, "I told you so." And Al never said nothing either. As for me, I was ahorseback again, no car, no cows, no money, busted all ways.

Some years later, Grandma told me something about the day I'd shipped my cattle off. She had this pair of field glasses, and she said she'd watched me as I waited with my little herd on the other side of Smith Lake for Kelly and his stock truck.

"I felt so sad," she said. "There you were with that bunch of cattle grazing there in that little open spot. You were sitting down under a shade tree, holding your horse.

"I thought to myself, if only he knew what the hell he was doing."

I suppose it's the nature of the young to do foolish things. And I suppose there are times when the best a parent can do is watch from a distance.

Forty-nine Wild Roses

Old Al probably never heard of Charles Darwin, but he sure believed in the survival of the fittest. If anything on our place was strong enough or quick enough or smart enough to live until it could breed, then it got to pass on its strength or speed or brains. But if it wasn't able to make it until then on its own, Old Al just let it die.

This rough philosophy was imprinted onto my brains from the first days I was big enough to ride out with him. I remember one day when I was eight, we were riding through the fields and we came upon a newborn colt, a weak little guy struggling to get up on its feet. I hopped off of Gypsy to give it a hand.

"Just leave that son-of-a-bitch alone," Old Al said.

"But it's weak," I pleaded.

"Just leave it alone," he repeated. "You save that son-of-a-bitch and it'll have a colt, and that one'll be weak, too. If it gets up, it gets up. If it don't, it'll die."

I went back a couple of hours later and the colt was dead.

Old Al liked being surrounded by animals that were survivors. He'd say, "If you start babyin' 'em, you're gonna make welfare cases out of 'em, and you'll have somethin' you'll have to take care of the rest of your life."

This attitude developed in Old Al during the tough times he'd gone through, like the years when he didn't have enough hay crop, and, by God, those years you just had to have cattle that would survive. The attitude had been built into him by harsh experience, and he held to it even through times that were good, because you never knew when your fortune would change. With him, survival was a habit, a way of life, something to be practiced until it became natural.

So in winter when we were short of hay, Old Al's cattle learned to follow the horses around as they pawed through the snow to uncover grass. And they'd go where cattle normally didn't go to find their food in summer, because Al's range wasn't always the best. I'd hear the neighbors remark, "Look at them Neas cattle up there on top of that ridge. I've never seen cattle up there this time of year, it bein' as hot as it is."

Al never vaccinated his cattle, but they never seemed to get sick with the typical diseases cows get. It wasn't until I was older that I realized there were diseases, like blackleg, that could kill a cow. Al's admonition was, "Don't start doctorin' the sons-of-bitches."

He thought it was really crazy for a man to get up in the middle of the night to check his cows during calving time, even though it was a common and prudent practice. A rancher would bring his cows in close when they were due and watch over them and get up several times during the night to make sure the calves were being born with no trouble. Sometimes a man would have to pull a calf, or turn it around, or in extreme situations, haul the cow to the vet for a Cesarean section. Or maybe the newborn calf would need to be brought into a warming shed in severe weather, or even into the house where it needed human help to make it through the night.

But none of Old Al's cows got pampered like that. We had a neighbor who got up routinely during the night to check on things at calving time, and I remember Old Al saying, "Well, I'll be a son-of-a-bitch! That man layin' there beside a woman gets out of bed in the middle of the night to go out to check a cow, for Christ's sake, to see if she can have a calf! I've never heard of anything so dumb in my life. Who in the hell'd *do* that?"

You might think Old Al would lose more than his share of cattle, but the truth is, he lost damn few. I remember one heifer who got to lying down with her back downhill while she was calving, and she died because a cow can't get up unless it can get its feet under itself, which it can't do with its back downhill. They can't roll into the proper position. They just lie there helpless, and when that happens they eventually drown in their own body fluids.

So Al lost that heifer that I remember, but not many more. He simply didn't lose calves like you hear about today. Maybe he really had bred strength into his herd over the years, by letting the weak die their natural death, and by letting the ones who were strong and resistant to disease, the easy calvers, and the good food-scroungers survive and pass on what they had in their makeup to their young.

Al liked Shorthorn cows. He always said the only time Shorthorn blood will hurt you is when there isn't enough of it. He didn't like just any Shorthorns, they had to be roan cows with spots of color against a white background. They could be red roans or blue roans, he didn't care, but he loved them spotted cattle. I always thought they were ugly bastards, and I still do, and so did most of our neighbors. I mean, why would a man own a bunch of cows that all looked different, all spotted in odd ways, when he could have Black Angus or Herefords or something that had some uniformity to it, so when he looked out over his herd in the evening he'd see beauty in the orderliness of what he had created?

Old Al was the only rancher around who had them spotted Shorthorns, except for one neighbor, Faye Burgess, who also loved spotted cows. Him and Old Al got along real good, and Al bought spotted bulls from Faye and kept his line pure.

The reason Old Al liked Shorthorns is that they were terrific milkers, not for us to use the milk or sell it, but for their own calves. You'd see a Shorthorn calf taking milk from its mother and there'd be a pile of foam on the ground at its feet. It'd be sucking hard, and the milk would be flowing so strong it would run out the sides of its mouth and make a bubbly puddle on the ground, and that cow had plenty more where that come from, and it's the milk that makes the calf, Old Al would always say.

The other thing Al liked about Shorthorns was their build. He was really big on conformation in an animal, be it a cow or a horse. What he liked about the Shorthorns was they were big, tall cattle, and they were long, "horsy" he used to call them, big frames with their brisket high off the ground.

For a while there was a movement to produce short, fat cattle. They called them "compress" cows, because everything was compressed into a tight package, less leg, less bone, short, squat cows supposedly with more meat, a very efficient sort of cow. That was the idea, anyway. Old Al never believed it would work. He felt the bigger the frame, the more meat a man could hang off of it. "You got a little frame," he'd say, "you can't put nothin' on it." Makes sense, don't it? Not only that, but the cows on his place needed long legs to get out and travel to look for food.

So the only cows on our place were roan-colored Shorthorns. And his particular, prejudiced eye for color extended to horses, too. The only horses Al kept were sorrels or bays.

Old Al didn't like Palomino horses. And he hated Pintos.

"Them cayuse sons-of bitches," he'd say. "I'd ride an Appaloosa before I'd ride a Pinto."

But it wasn't just color he was hung up on. It mattered a lot the way a horse was built.

He liked the head on an Arabian real well, but he said there was no conformation to those horses, all they was ever bred for was that head, the breeders never looked at the ass of the horse. If the Arabian horse people had a colt born and he had that beautiful head, no matter if he was so cow-hocked his hocks were rubbing together, they'd leave the nuts in him, and it hurt their breed. Some of those horses had great color and a beautiful head, but when you'd seen that, you'd seen it all.

Old Al had the same feeling about Thoroughbred blood in his horses as he did about Shorthorn blood in his cows. He'd say the only time Thoroughbred blood will hurt you is when there isn't enough of it. He didn't like a pure Thoroughbred, because they were too hot for ranch work. But he liked the way a Thoroughbred had high, strong withers to hang a saddle on. But he also wanted a horse with a big rear end, lots of muscles to set back on and drive ahead with, lots of power in the rear to jump out and turn a cow.

And every one of Old Al's horses had a soft mouth. All horses are born with soft mouths. Whether they keep them or not depends on how they're broke, and how they're treated as they're growing up. It depends, really, on the philosophy and skill of the trainer.

Old Al had the most tender hands on a horse's mouth of any man I ever saw. He could stop his horses with just a backward tick on the reins, and turn them one way or the other with the flick of one pinky. "Stay out of that horse's face!" he'd yell at me when I was leaning on the reins too hard, because the more you worked away on a horse's mouth, the tougher it got, and the harder it was to control him in the end.

Old Al never used a curb chain under the horse's chin to put pressure on the sensitive nerves there, just a piece of leather, and he never used a tie-down to keep the horse from tossing its head. Old Al said, "If a horse don't have a mouth, he ain't got nothin'." And he would train his horses from the start to be responsive and to tuck their heads under so they could look down at the cattle in front of them, especially when he made them stop. I don't have the soft hands he did, and I've seen damn few men who do, damn few who could ride a horse with such gentleness and ease, or train it with such patience and care.

But what really fascinated me about Old Al was how he could be mean to a horse. If a horse wanted to fight him, he'd abuse the bastard.

This rarely happened with a horse Al had raised, but he also brought a whole bunch of horses home that nobody could ride, most of them from Moore's dude ranch outside of Kila. They'd hire Old Al to castrate their colts and offer to pay him twenty dollars for the job. Instead, he'd offer to take a couple of outlaw horses off their hands, mean, counterfeit bastards who'd bucked off all the dudes and all the ranch hands, too, older horses that knew better but were just ornery and rotten and dangerous.

It was usually a good deal for Old Al, because once he'd reminded those horses about their manners, he could sell them for a hundred dollars apiece. It was better money than he got for cutting colts, and he needed it.

When Old Al rode one of them renegades, he always carried a eight-foot piece of hard twist rope, doubled over. At the first sign of trouble, Al would whip the horse on the butt and the hind legs and then down under between the legs, over and under, one side after the other, repeatedly. "This horse needs its dink hare-lipped," he'd say, and he wouldn't stop until he'd raised welts an inch high.

He'd never abuse a colt, or an older horse that was trying to learn. But a horse who knew better and was trying to get away with something or was being mean, well, then Old Al knew what to do.

To start with, he'd take a bad horse and tie him up short in the hot sun, with the saddle on and cinched up tight. He'd leave him out there for six or eight hours, just standing there, no water or nothing, and that would take a lot of the fight out of him for that day.

And then he'd put some of them out on what he called a stake rope. Picture this: here's this horse, ten, twelve years old. He's bucked every cowboy in the damn country off. He's just a dirty, miserable, counterfeit son-of-a-bitch. But still a pretty good-looking horse, so once you got him to going O.K., you could sell him.

This horse is fighting every way he can, so Al'd put him on what he called a stake rope. He'd tie a really stout rope about a hundred feet long to the horse's halter, and tie the other end to the bottom of a big post. Then he'd deliberately spook the horse. That horse would take off running, and when he'd hit the end of the rope, it'd snap his neck around and flip him on the ground. The horse'd get up and take off in another direction, and when he hit the end of the rope again, same thing would happen.

After a while, them horses would get to know where the end of that rope was. Al'd spook one, and he'd run off, but he'd stop just short of having his head jerked off. But Old Al knew how to handle that.

There was one particularly miserable mare he'd got who'd learned where the end of the rope was after a couple of treatments. One day, she was standing there, loafing in the shade, and Old Al snuck up and drug in about thirty feet of that rope and tied it off to the post.

"Now watch this old bitch," he said to me, and he run around and throwed his hat at her. The horse took off.

By now, she'd learned she could run a hundred feet and still be O.K., but this time, after about seventy feet that rope came to an abrupt end, and snap, whap, down on the ground she went.

This was really rotten, hard treatment, and he could have broken the necks of these horses. But there was no working with them until he'd got through to them, and to do that he had to be meaner than they were, and they had to know it.

He had another setup he used which he called a draw rein. What he'd do is, he'd tie a lariat rope to the saddle horn. Then he'd run the rope from the horn through the ring in the snaffle bit he'd put in their mouth, and he'd hang onto the end of the rope. Then he'd spook them and make them run away. Just before they hit the end of the rope, he'd wrap it around his hip and sit down on it. That would jerk their mouth right back to the saddle horn. Jeeze, their neck would bend back there quick, and they'd flop down on the ground, hard.

One time he brought an Appaloosa horse back to the place who'd strike at you with his front feet and do anything else he could to hurt you, he was so dirty and rotten. Al threw him with the draw rein, and then he run up and tied his head fast to the saddle horn and left him lying there in the sun for two hours.

After that, he got him up and said, "Now we'll kink your neck the other way, you son-of-a-bitch," and he turned his head to the other side, tied it down by the saddle horn again, and left him there for a couple hours more. The next day he was riding him. The horse had finally said, "The hell with it," and quit.

But Al didn't like doing that to an animal. He told me, "You're breakin' their spirit, you're takin' their spirit away from 'em," and I could tell it went against everything he believed about training horses the right way from the day they were old enough to learn. None of the horses whose spirits he'd broke stayed on our ranch. He sold them as soon as he could.

But these times were tough, these years of the Great Depression, and if Old Al had to change his ways some of the time to sell a horse here and there to get by and provide for his family, so be it. Like old Darwin said, adapt or die.

So this Grandpa of mine, Old Al, my idol, remained throughout my boyhood a contradiction. The man with the most gentle of hands on a horse's mouth could also slam one into the ground and leave him tied down for hours in the hot sun. And I always felt Old Al was most understanding about a small boy's needs, but he never put up with open displays of affection.

He never hugged me, and I never once was allowed to crawl up on his lap, nor was I permitted to call him "Grandpa."

"My name is Al," he'd say sternly.

I can't remember him ever putting his arm around

Grandma or giving her a kiss. Every once in a while, he'd slap her on the ass when he walked by, but that was as far as he'd ever go. And he never bought her a present, not even at Christmas, not one in their whole time together, and I know that because Grandma told me.

She once pointed out to him that he never told her that he loved her.

"I told you I loved you the day we were married," he replied. "If I ever quit, I'll let you know."

There was just one departure from this aloofness of his, and it took place every June 17th, the anniversary of their wedding. When Old Al came in from working on that day, he'd have a wild rose in his hatband. He'd take it in his hand and hold it out to her, not saying a word. He did this every June 17th from as far back as I can remember until the year he died. In all, he and Grandma were married forty-nine years, and she said he brought her forty-nine roses he had picked out on the range.

She kept them in her Bible until they crumbled and turned to dust.

A Love Story

When Al Neas wanted to take the girl who became my Grandma out on a date in 1898, he had to swim his horse across the Snake River in Idaho to get her. He was holding a herd of horses on the other side, so they had to swim back, the girl kneeling on the horse's rump behind him with her skirts hiked up to keep them clear of the water.

Al was thirty and Ruth Ella Williams was sixteen, a bit of a spread in years, but he had never married, and she'd had her heart set on this man she called "the handsome buckaroo" since the first time she'd seen him, two years earlier.

That was at what they called a celebration in those days, what we call a rodeo now. They had a big gray horse there who'd bucked everybody off and they were offering fifty dollars to anybody who could get him rode. Al said he'd give it a try.

"He rode him so easy," Grandma would say. "He made him look sick." And she admired him from that day.

Much of Al's life up to that point had prepared him for that ride. He had been a true kid of the West in the second half of the 1800s, a tough kid, self-sufficient early in life, getting nothing the easy way. His mother had died when he was little, and by the time he was nine, Al was driving a team of oxen for his father, old Pete Neas, who hauled freight. Before that, Pete had run a Pony Express station near the White Desert in Utah.

Pete Neas was a huge man from a family of huge people. They say that one time he and his three sisters got on a scale together and it topped a thousand pounds. His exploits as a station keeper earned him a place in the book, *The Pony Express Goes Through*, mostly for his toughness.

They tell one story about the night he suspected Indians were going to raid his station. Instead of boarding things up and hunkering down behind some barrel, Pete Neas went out to the corral after dark, plucked a post out of the ground, and stood there in its place, waiting. Pretty soon an Indian come sneaking by, and old Pete put a bullet in his back.

So my Grandpa come from real western stock, and there he was at age nine, driving nine yoke of oxen. There's two oxen to a yoke, so this little kid handled a team of eighteen pulling a freight wagon along, with men driving three other teams. Oxen are slow, but they pull hard and are easy to handle and won't run off. They had seventy-two oxen in all in Pete Neas's freight outfit, and one saddle horse they would use to round up the oxen in the morning. That was a job Pete gave to young Al.

Every morning when the men were preparing breakfast, Al was sent out to round up the oxen that had been turned loose to graze during the night. And every morning when he got back, the breakfast was all eaten up, except for some bacon grease in the frying pan, which he'd wipe up with a hunk of bread. He was hungry all the time, so at age nine, Al took up smoking because it killed his appetite.

Two years of that was about all a kid could take, so Al left his father and struck out on his own. He wound up in the Flathead Valley of Montana in 1879, an eleven-year-old kid on a horse he probably stole, with ten cents in his pocket. He bought a dime's worth of hay for his horse, fed him half of it, and slept on the rest. In the morning he fed the other half to the horse, then set out looking for work.

There was this guy from Nebraska around who had a big herd of three- and four-year-old steers up at Browning on good grass. He was putting together a crew to trail them out of Montana Territory. Al had heard about it, so he pulled his hat down as low as it would go, put a cigarette in his mouth, and went in and asked the man for a job.

"How old are ya?" asked the boss.

"Twenty-one," said Al.

The boss reached over and pulled his hat up and said, "The hell ya are!"

But he gave him a job anyway, on the chuck wagon, chopping wood and helping out. Just a few days out on the trail the boss realized he was a mite short of hands, so Al wound up riding drag and pulling down full wages.

This was the kid who grew up to be the man who could ride the bucking horse at the celebration and catch the fancy of a fourteen-year-old girl. After that day, Ruth Ella didn't see her "handsome buckaroo" for another two years. Then, once again, it was a bucking horse that brought them together.

By then, Al had linked up with her brother, Joe Williams, another rough cowboy. He was a real small man, and people often called him Little Joe. Later, he would become something of an outlaw, but for now, he was doing honest work with Al, breaking horses for a man named Tom Lander, in Freemont County, Idaho. Joe was up on a real mean bronc one day in April, and this horse went over backwards with him, smashed him up real bad, and they sent for his family.

Ruth Ella and her mother drove over in a buggy with the doctor. Joe was so busted up they had to haul him home, and since the buggy was small, they had to leave Ruth Ella behind. To get back home, she could walk, or ride Joe's horse, Cigar.

She chose to ride, and as she headed out, Al turned to one of his buddies and said, "I should go with that girl. Cigar is a stampeder."

By that he meant this rotten horse would take the bit in his teeth and run away. He'd even done it with Al himself once, tearing off through the sagebrush and badger holes. Al said that when the horse finally stopped, he pulled his saddle off "the loco bastard" and turned him loose. Anytime a cowboy chooses to *walk* back to camp, you know he was on a *real* bad horse.

But Al didn't go with her for some reason, and sure enough Cigar took the bit and, as Ruth Ella put it, "went out over rough country like a bullet." He stopped once to get his wind, then took off again, finally running all the way back to the home ranch. Ruth Ella was so shaken she went to bed and stayed there for a week.

"That was the first heart attack I ever had," she said later. "With Joe hurt and me not able to help Mother, she had a bad time with the two of us down and out."

But the silver lining was that the incident brought Al around to see how she and Joe were doing. Al was still angry about the horse, and told her to "stay off the son-of-a-bitch."

"He'll kill ya," Al said. "Joe should kill *him*. There's too many good horses around to put up with somethin' like that."

But Joe didn't kill Cigar, and in fact, he continued to ride him, which worked out O.K. for Ruth Ella, who often got to ride along as Al and Joe "chummed around."

This was during Joe Williams' calmer years. Later, he would become a wanted man. His family still tells the story about the family gunfight near Mud Lake, Idaho in 1913. Joe had teamed up with a man named Sam Thomas, also known as Scarface. When Sam was a little boy, he had tipped a pail full of lye off the kitchen table onto his head, the caustic lye spilling all over his face, scarring his appearance and maybe his attitude as well.

Anyway, Joe's brother Bill suspected the two of them of rustling some horses he owned, and he wanted them back. He asked his brother-in-law Mose Johnson to ride along with him because he expected trouble, and Mose agreed. This Mose Johnson was one hell of a hand with a pistol. By all accounts, he was a gentle man who was quiet and loving with his family, but when he was riled, you wanted to be on his side. Al had cowboyed with him, and said Mose Johnson was the most absolutely dangerous man he'd ever met.

Well, off they went to get Bill's horses back. When they confronted Joe and Scarface, things really started popping. Scarface drew his gun and pulled the trigger three times, and each time it misfired. All the while, he was trying to shield himself behind his horse, but it did no good. Mose and Bill both cut loose, killing the horse *and* Scarface.

Joe took off a-running, and Mose would have killed him dead if Bill hadn't hit his arm away as he fired, in what might have been a gesture of brotherly love. Joe made it around the side of the house, hopped on Mose's horse, and took off, a horse thief once again, but still a free man.

The law almost got him once. He was on the lam when one of his children died. Joe loved his family, and the authorities knew it and knew he wouldn't pass up the funeral, so they had it staked out real good. As they scanned the crowd for Joe, they overlooked a short woman mourner dressed in black. It was, of course, Little Joe come to bury his child.

So, this was the nature of my Grandma's family, rough-and-tumble as Al's had been, cowhands and gun hands, one of them an outlaw, all of them very much western. Despite the age difference, a match between Al Neas and Ruth Ella Williams seemed to be right in background and temperament. But it almost didn't have time to come together.

One day in the spring of 1898, a big outfit called the Diamond A from Oregon passed through Freemont County, Idaho with a trail herd of horses. They were looking for hands, and Al signed on. He told Ruth Ella, sixteen years old and in love, that he'd be gone for a very long time, and off he rode.

Ruth Ella moped around for three days, so sad she said she felt "indigo blue." Then off in the distance she saw a rider plunging his horse across the Snake River, heading toward her. Al, it seems, couldn't take the separation, either, so back he came and took the job holding the horse herd on the opposite bank.

That fall, he asked her to marry him.

"Girl," he said, "you are the first girl I ever saw that I wanted to spend the rest of my life with, and will you?"

"Yes," replied Ruth Ella, "if Father and Mother will permit."

"If they permit, will you marry me?"

"Yes, if they do, I will."

"Will you stay with me always?"

"If I marry you, I will stay with you until the end of the trail."

"Well," said Al, "that's long enough."

At some point during that day, he confessed to her his mighty secret. They would never have children, because he had only one testicle.

Grandma may have swallowed hard at this news—she never said—but since she was as long on love as they were short on medical knowledge, it made no matter.

But what of Al? This tough and handsome cowboy, this rider of rough stock, what had this awful secret done to him through the years? Was this why he had remained unwed until his thirties? What turmoil had he endured the day he asked the young Ruth Ella to accept him?

They were married on June 17, 1899. Al drove her to her wedding in an Overland stagecoach, she inside with her mother and sister Kitty, him up in the box, handling the long lines himself. The last week of that month, they rode out of Idaho and into Montana, heading for the Klondike, way up north, where they'd heard there was gold for the taking. They drove eighteen head of horses before them, selling one here and there along the way as they needed money to live on.

They stopped for the winter in the Bears Paw Mountains of Montana where Al got a job breaking horses at a ranch. Their home was a sheepherder's dugout, kind of like a cave dug into the side of a hill, but with walls and a ceiling of boards.

It soon became apparent that Al's fears about his ability to reproduce were unfounded, and Ruth Ella went into labor the first week in March. Her mother was with them at the time, on a visit, and that was fortunate, because it's unlikely that Al would have been able to handle what happened by himself.

His young bride, now eighteen years old, was in labor in the one-room dugout for more than twenty-four hours. For most of that time, part of her baby's head protruded from her womb, stuck there. Eventually, the boy was born. Ruth Ella lay still, her eyes rolled back in her head, paralyzed. It appeared as if she would die.

Later that spring, they bundled up their new baby and rode out of the Bears Paw Mountains, heading north once again.

More than thirty years later, I would come to live with them, and they would take me in and raise me. I would know them as Old Al and Grandma. But that was a ways ahead, and then they still had the dreams and trails of their own youth to follow.

Mountain View

The yellow stallion was having a bit of trouble keeping the wolves away from his mares, but so far he was holding them off.

He'd bunched the mares and their colts and he circled around to hold them tight, and whenever a wolf got too close he'd kick at him, or strike at him with his front hooves. Al watched this scene for a while across the fields of snow, then turned to his young bride and said, "By God, I'd like to have that horse. I'm gonna crease him." He ran off at a crouch for a ways, then he got down on his belly and began crawling across the open fields, his rifle in his right hand.

Al had seen an old Englishman catch wild horses by "creasing" them. He'd never tried it himself, but the Englishman had enormous success doing it, and it seemed easy enough. The Englishman could make it work every time.

What he'd do was shoot the horse just ahead of its withers,

just about a quarter inch down into the flesh under the mane, no more. The dorsal spines on the backbone of a horse stick way up about there, and the punch of the bullet going through so nearby would set them twanging. The shock waves vibrating up and down the spinal cord would knock the horse out cold for a few minutes, just long enough for the Englishman to run up and tie its feet together, and then he'd have him.

So there went Al Neas, crawling off through the snow toward the Palomino stallion he wanted so bad, toward the mares and the colts and the wolves. Ruth Ella watched all this unfold before her in the cold of the Alberta winter, watched her new husband creeping along until he came to a fallen tree, where he raised up his shoulders, poked his rifle over the top, and laid the iron sights on the very uppermost edge of the stallion's neck.

"Ka-BOOM!"

Down went the stallion and off went the mares, their colts close behind. The wolves lit out in another direction, and Al was on his feet and moving before any of them got over the next hill. He could tie down a horse faster than any man around, and he raced up to that stallion and had all fours tied as fast as he'd ever done it in his life. Then he stood back and waited.

He waited longer than he figured a man would have to wait for a creased horse to recover. It eventually dawned on him that he was alone under the gray winter sky with a dead horse, its feet all tied up. It was a long trudge back through the snow to where his wife was waiting.

They had abandoned their plans for the Klondike and its fortunes, perhaps because what they found when they crossed the border into Southern Alberta in 1900 was inviting enough. It was a land of endless grass and abundant water, with the Rocky Mountains on its western flank. The town of Cardston had been settled some thirteen years earlier by Mormons looking for a new home, and since then hundreds more had come up the trail from Utah in covered wagons. In 1900, the population was about three thousand.

The town had a weekly newspaper, *The Cardston Record*, and the year Al and Ruth Ella pulled in, the paper's editor, Norman W. McLeod, wrote a small book about the area, which he described as "unrivaled among the stock countries of the world." This guy wrote that the grass was so plentiful that "there are countless herds of fat cattle on the ranges of Southern Alberta which, at any season, are neither fed nor sheltered." A man could let a cow eat grass for four years and then sell it off the range for forty dollars.

As for horses, McLeod wrote:

Alberta occupies a somewhat similar position to Canada that Kentucky does to the United States. Owing to the high altitude, the dry and invigorating atmosphere, short and mild winters, and its nutritious grasses and inexhaustible supply of clear, cold water, it is preeminently adapted for breeding horses, and the Alberta animal has already become noted for endurance, lung power and perfect freedom from hereditary and other diseases.

A man could sell a good horse in that country for as much as one hundred dollars.

This little booklet ended with an invitation

to all people to come to Southern Alberta. . . . in the language of the Holy Writ, 'a land of brooks of water, of fountains and depths that spring out of valleys and hills; a land wherein thou shall eat bread without scarceness; thou shall not lack anything in it.' It is the promised land.

To Al Neas, with his young wife and his infant son, with his small herd of horses, and his abilities and his strong back, this sounded pretty good. What's more, there was land for the taking. A man could homestead 160 acres for a ten dollar filing fee and an oath of allegiance to the Canadian government, a government eager enough for settlers from the United States that it allowed them to bring their household possessions and tools and farm equipment across the border duty-free, along with sixteen head of stock.

The only down side for Al was all those Mormons. Al wasn't big on religion, Mormons in particular, and this was definitely one place where it looked like he'd be one of the few people who wasn't a member of the church. He'd be an outsider. What saved it, for Ruth Ella at least, was the curious fact that Cardston also had a Presbyterian minister. He was Gavin Hamilton, and he had arrived in town three years earlier. Ruth Ella was the granddaughter of a Presbyterian minister and a faithful churchgoer even if Al wasn't, so maybe the little Neas family might fit in after all.

They settled near the small town of Mountain View in the foothills of the Rockies, seventeen miles from Cardston, and Al Neas soon established his reputation as a horseman. He went to work for the great Cochrane Ranch, at that time the largest cattle ranch in the world, and there they learned before long that he could ride anything nobody else could handle.

This reputation had its pluses and its minuses. It was a fine way to get established in a new land, but after a while Al's working string was made up of horses that had bucked other cowboys off. A rider would complain about a horse to Alexander Flemming, the foreman, who'd say, "Well, take him over and put him in Al's string."

One particularly rotten son-of-a-bitch that wound up in "the dirty string" was a big horse from Oregon named Traveler, half Thoroughbred, mean as could be, and nobody could ride him, or even wanted to try. He bucked Al off three times in one hour. The first time, the horse threw Al so high he landed on his knees behind the saddle. The second time he got thrown way clear, and the third time, he landed on his feet standing beside the horse. After that, they got along fine.

One evening, a young cowboy walked up to the bunkhouse carrying his saddle, and he started immediately bragging about what a good rider he was, about how he could ride anything they had on the ranch. Flemming didn't need any more hands at that time, and said so, but that didn't stop this young cowboy. His name was Charlie Van Cleeve, and he bragged away about himself through dinner, and that night when the men were bedded down and trying to get to sleep, he was still yakking away about how good he was. At breakfast he started in again.

Flemming had had about enough of this, so he told Al, "Go get that roan horse. We'll kill this son-of-a-bitch right now."

Van Cleeve got on him and the horse started bucking. He didn't run around the corral, he bucked his way around it, Van Cleeve hanging on and smiling. When they bucked their way past Flemming, Van Cleeve reached around to the horse's chest and yanked out a fistful of hair, threw it in the air at the foreman, and cried, "How do you like him?"

Flemming pounded his saddle horn in rage, shouting, "You're hired, you son-of-a-bitch, you're hired!"

Al said Charlie Van Cleeve was the best rider he'd ever seen, and they became good friends. Charlie got married a short time later. One evening, he and his wife were driving home in a buggy when the front wheel hit a rock. The jolt threw Van Cleeve out, and he was killed.

Two things were becoming clear for Al Neas during those years in Southern Alberta after the turn of the century. First, he would make his reputation and his fortune—if you could call it that—as a horseman. He tried his hand at farming, and he raised cattle, good cattle that brought in money, and some other livestock. But he was never as good at any of those things as he was with horses.

The second thing to become clear was that his earlier fears about being unable to produce offspring were entirely groundless. The birth of the little boy Leslie in the Bear Paw Mountains had surprised him and reassured him about his manhood, but then the babies started coming along with predictable regularity. Pretty soon there was Lil, and then Howard, and then Violet, and then Bernice, and then Hazel, and the Neas homestead was filling up.

Al always made money to feed all those mouths one way or another, usually from the back of a horse. He broke a lot of horses for stockmen in the area and helped gather up rough stock for the first Calgary Stampede. And he and some of his cronies broke horses to sell to the British cavalry, which needed to mount its troops for the Boer War.

They would trail the horses to Fort Macleod and sell them to the English officers at the remount corrals there. After one such trip, Al and Jim Austin and Grant Short and some others were heading for home. Austin was riding a horse the English buyers had rejected. Suddenly, it started bucking, and then turned a complete somersault, landing with Austin underneath.

"Jim's deader'n a mackerel," said Al.

But they got the horse off his body, and took off his boots, and poured whiskey down his throat. It didn't have any effect, and the other riders standing around took off their hats. At that point, the corpse opened its eyes and said, "Son-of-a-bitch! Why'd you waste all that whiskey? I'm wet as a fish!"

After such adventures, Al would come home and throw a roll of money on the kitchen table and say, "Girl, that'll keep us ahead of the hounds for a while." He also made some money selling horses to people around Mountain View, like the blind horse he sold to the preacher.

Al didn't like preachers and he didn't trust them, so when this preacher drove his buggy up to the barn and said he was looking for a gentle horse, Al was ready for him. He had a real pretty two-year-old that was just sweet as could be, mostly because he'd hung around the barnyard all his life and the kids had played with him every day. He was really nice looking and as gentle as any preacher would want. Only thing was, he was blind.

When this preacher said he wanted a gentle horse, Al brought this one out and led him around, and let the preacher pet him. The deal was settled, and the preacher tied his new horse to the back of his buggy and trotted off down the lane, and when he came to the main road, he stopped for a moment. His new horse, trotting along behind, had no idea the buggy had stopped, and kept coming. This buggy had a nice cloth covering over the cab, and when the buggy stopped the young horse ran right into the back of it, busting his head through the cloth cover.

"What the hell's the matter with you?" shouted the preacher. "You blind or somethin'?"

And then there was the Englishman who wanted a buggy team in a hurry. Al heard about it and needed the money, but he didn't have a team trained to drive. So he hitched up two horses he was willing to part with, two horses who had never pulled anything before. One of them was named Eagle Ribs, because of the way his ribs stuck out. Neither of these horses liked the idea a whole lot, and it looked like it might be pretty shaky convincing the Englishman they were a real team. That's when Al decided to make Ruth Ella drive.

She didn't want any part of it, but Al assured her that the "team" wouldn't try leaving the road because of the trees on either side.

"And I'll be up ahead on my horse with my rope," he said. "If they run away, I'll snag 'em as they go past."

With this reassurance, off they went. The Englishman liked the way they came into the yard, so proud-looking and spirited, and said he'd take them.

"Are you sure you can handle 'em?" asked Al.

"I can drive anything a woman can!" replied the Englishman, and the deal was made. The first time he took his new team out, Eagle Ribs figured he'd had enough of being a buggy horse, reared up, fell over backwards, and landed on the seat alongside his new owner.

One day a traveling piano salesman came through Mountain View, trying to drum up some business. Al knew that Ruth Ella had always wanted a piano, although he couldn't understand why, since nobody in the family could play one. But she wanted a piano in her parlor real bad, for whatever sense of position it gave her, so he told the salesman he couldn't afford to buy one, but he'd be willing to trade some horses for one. Horseflesh being as valuable as it was in those days, the piano salesman said, "You bet!" In the end, they agreed on a piano for ten horses. Later that day, the salesman was bragging about his deal to the clerk in the town store.

"I just traded one piano for ten horses!" he said.

"Really?" said the clerk. "Who'd ya trade with?"

"Fella named Al Neas," said the piano salesman.

The clerk nodded. "You seen these horses yet?" he asked.

"Nope. But he guarantees they're all sound!"

That's about all they were. For one piano for his wife's parlor, Al had traded away ten of the worst outlaws and counterfeit bastards on the place, rejects from his other deals, horses so bad he couldn't unload them and didn't want to have to feed them.

He'd exchanged horses nobody wanted to ride for a piano nobody could play.

As the years went by, it became apparent that things were not quite right with Leslie, the little boy whose birth in the Bear Paw Mountains had almost killed Ruth Ella. He'd seemed fine for a while, but as he got older they noticed that his eyes were very weak and they twitched from side to side constantly in a flickering movement. He couldn't keep up in school, and didn't play as the other children did. Ruth Ella had taken him to doctors without satisfaction, and now, when he was eleven, she decided it was time to take him to a specialist in Victoria.

The doctor examined Leslie and announced that his eyes would never improve, and that his mind had been affected by his rough beginning as well. He would never, said the specialist, be able to perform beyond the level of an eight year old. There was nothing he could do for the young mother and her son, said the doctor, except to recommend that, for the boy's own good, he be castrated, an operation to which Ruth Ella reluctantly consented.

Before returning to Mountain View, Ruth Ella took Leslie to a concert at the Opera House, for a treat. Then they returned to their ranch in the foothills of the Rockies, to the brother and sisters and to Al, to the house with the new piano in the parlor.

And Leslie sat on the stool before the keyboard and played back the Victoria symphony, note for note.

Big Bar Creek

When Al walked into the old trapper's cabin and looked on the kitchen table, he was shocked. In the place where he'd expected to find the deed to 160 acres of wheat land, there was a pine cone.

The old man who'd sold him the land was honest, Al had thought, and he'd promised to leave the deed behind when he pulled out. But now he was gone, and there was no deed in the cabin, a cabin that had been cleared and swept clean. There was nothing left but the wooden table in the bare room, and the pine cone on it.

The deal had been struck mighty quickly and without the usual formalities. Al and his brother Andrew had been out working the land they leased from the old-timer when a man from the city in a new car stopped by the ranch house. He asked Ruth Ella how to find the trapper's cabin, because he'd heard he had land to sell and he was there to buy it. Ruth Ella gave him directions. Then it dawned on her he was about to buy the fields where Al and Andrew grew their wheat.

In a panic, she put Leslie on a horse and told him to ride across the ridge and tell Al what was about to happen. She told him several times the precise words to repeat, and Leslie nodded that he understood. He must have, too, because by the time the city man got to the trapper's place in his car, Al had arrived on a lathered horse, and sealed his own hurried deal to buy the land he needed to keep his family afloat.

But now some weeks later, he stood in the empty cabin, staring at the table where the deed should have been. Gone was the old man, gone was Al's money, and instead of the paper that would secure the family's future, there was a pine cone. It was as if the trapper had played a cruel trick as he closed the door and headed down the road, laughing. Then Al saw the rat droppings.

On a hunch, he picked up the pine cone and put a penny from his pocket on the table in its place. The next day, the penny was gone, and on the table there was a small stick. Al knew what he was dealing with now, and it wasn't the deceit of an old man. It was a trade rat.

A trade rat is kind of like a pack rat, but it doesn't collect stuff to store away in its nest. A trade rat likes to swap things, and every time it takes something, it leaves something else in return. This particular rat had seen the deed on the table and traded a pine cone for it. Then it had traded a stick for the penny. Al could have searched a year and never found the rat's nest, so his only hope of getting the deed to his new property was to keep trading for it. With luck, the rat would eventually turn it over.

And two weeks later, it did.

Al now owned 160 acres of dry wheat land on Big Bar Mountain, in the Cariboo District of British Columbia, a little ways from the Fraser River and most of a day's ride from the little town of Clinton. He owned some bottomland along Big Bar Creek, too, and he was busy raising his wheat and pigs and horses and cattle—and kids, who now numbered ten.

It was Ruth Ella who had insisted on the move from the ranch in southern Alberta, the land of plenty. The problem was, despite the heavy Mormon presence in the country around Cardston, Al was able to find plenty of whiskey to drink, and drink it he did, often staying away several days at a time.

"I met Old John Seagram," he'd tell Ruth Ella when he returned. "Couldn't get away."

For a long time, Ruth Ella thought he was talking about an old friend, and later she said, "I thought Old John Seagram sure must have what it takes to keep Al away so long."

But she found out the truth eventually, and saw Al heading down a path that would lead to his destruction and hers, so in 1913 she made them move to a place they'd heard about from friends, across the mountains to the west.

They went by train through the Canadian Rockies, past towering peaks spilling streams cold and white with the runoff of glaciers, then across the arid land of rolling sagebrush hills, past the long and narrow Shuswap Lake, to the town of Kamloops. From there, they went west further still, and then north to Clinton and beyond, past a wide spot in the road called Jesmond, and on to the banks of Big Bar Creek where it tumbled through a narrow valley toward the Fraser River.

This was isolated country, sparse in population and rugged. If Ruth Ella's goal was to insulate the family from the evil influences of the day, it seemed she had picked a likely spot.

It was also a place where a person had to learn to do for himself, because the flip side of isolation is self-sufficiency. There were some neighbors around, and a number of Indians, but when a problem arose, it was generally yours to deal with.

Big Bar Creek was spotted with homesteaders, and up on the mountain were the wheat fields of the few dryland farmers who were trying to make a go of it. Up there, too, was the great Gang Ranch, the biggest outfit in the Cariboo District, a ranch that ran many cows and employed a bunkhouse full of men to watch over them. Go to Clinton today and you can still hear the story of the time Old Al and Andrew met up with one of the riders from the Gang Ranch on the range.

Al and Andrew were down on their hands and knees,

butchering a beef cow they'd just killed, when the rider came upon them.

"What the hell you think you're doin'," he demanded.

"We're butcherin' this beef. What the hell's it look like we're doin'?" answered Al.

The Gang Ranch hand was obviously accusing them of stealing one of his outfit's cows. But there was no way he could prove it, because the part of the hide with the brand on it was out of sight, and he didn't want to press the matter because there was both Al and Andrew and just one of him, and accusing a man of rustling is serious business. So he let the matter rest and rode off. But that wasn't good enough for Andrew.

There was no way those Neas brothers liked being accused, justly or not, and they surely didn't want anybody making a habit of it. So old Andrew took the hide from the ass end of that cow down to the line cabin where this rider was staying, and he nailed it across his door. First he tacked the hide across the top, and then he stretched it tight as he could and nailed it on the bottom, so that right in the middle of that cowboy's door, right where he would look out upon the world, was the most insulting part of that cow's anatomy. It was a challenge that was never answered, and they heard nothing more about that beef or any other they killed on the range to feed Grandma and all them kids.

Word was getting out around the Cariboo District that

the Neas boys didn't have any back-up in their nature. There was this streak of toughness and righteousness that they didn't flaunt, and they didn't have to. It just sort of became apparent pretty soon that you could push a Neas just so far before you were sorry you'd started. My uncle Andrew stayed a bachelor all his days, and I always wondered why, until Grandma told me the story about the one fiancee he had, and how she'd crossed the line.

Grandma's attempts to isolate Old Al from John Seagram and his buddies didn't work, because one of the first ventures Al and Andrew got into with their new neighbors was the building of a clubhouse they called the Howling Dog Dance Hall. All the neighbors pitched in and made a barn raising of sorts out of it, and it was there the families from up and down Big Bar Creek and from up on the mountain would gather to let off their steam on Saturday night.

It was one of them genuine old-time country affairs, with the kids asleep on the benches while the folks danced to the fiddles and the men and a lot of the women drank home-made whiskey and raised a bit of hell. Andrew had linked up with the young schoolteacher who did her best to keep order in the community's one-room schoolhouse, and he'd given her a ring and they'd set the date, and everything was all set until the night he danced with the squaw.

There were a lot of Indians in the area, and they were a part of the crowd like everyone else, and they often showed up at the Howling Dog for their share of the fun. This particular Saturday night, Andrew asked one of the Indian ladies to dance with him. When he was done, his schoolteacher fiancee told him she never wanted him to dance with one of "those people" ever again.

That's all Andrew needed. He picked out the darkest Indian woman in the Howling Dog and danced with her all night long, and that was the end of his relationship with the schoolmarm. And there was never another woman in his life. But he valued his friends and his own sense of right and wrong more than he valued his one love.

A man needed to be sure of himself and his values to survive in those times in that place, because, like I said, often a man had to rely on himself alone, in matters big and small. Being sure and decisive and acting with confidence was a necessary habit.

This was particularly true in medical matters, because the doctor was usually a day's ride away or more, and he was expensive, too. In medical matters, Old Al was as rigid and self-confident as in anything in his life. He had enormous disdain for veterinarians, and he doctored his own animals, and he doctored his own family. And he used just three medicines on both: turpentine, pine tar, and sulfur.

The turpentine was an all-purpose disinfectant used on man and beast. As soon as one of the kids got a cut of any kind, Old Al would douse it with turpentine. It had remarkable properties, as I know from the later years, when he used it on me many times. First thing, it never stung when he poured it on, which surprised the hell out of me the first time he done it. Second, it took away the soreness. If you cut your hand, he just poured turpentine in the cut, and you could use that hand just fine with no pain.

But don't try repeating the treatment the next day. For reasons unknown to me, turpentine doesn't hurt when applied immediately, but it hurts like hell if you put it on again tomorrow.

Old Al was very particular about the turpentine he used, and not just any would do. After I came to live with them in Kila, I watched him buy all his turpentine from the Kalispell Mercantile, where they sold pure spirits of turpentine dipped from a wooden barrel. He'd take an empty whiskey bottle to town with him and he'd get a quart from the barrel. On the shelves were cans labeled "Pure Spirits of Turpentine," but Old Al said they were different, they were for thinning paint. He distrusted anything that didn't come in a wood container or in glass.

When he'd castrate a colt, he'd pour in the turpentine. And when one of the kids got cut playing along Big Bar Creek, turpentine was the answer.

Pine tar was his treatment for distemper in horses. If a horse had distemper, he'd isolate it from the rest, of course, then get a glob of pine tar on a stick. He'd reach in the horse's mouth and pull its tongue out as far as he could. The horse didn't appreciate this too much, naturally, and kicked up a bit, but Old Al would yank on that tongue until it was sticking way out. Then he'd reach back deep in the horse's throat with that stick and scrape off the glob of pine tar. When he let go of their tongue, they just naturally had to swallow, and down went the distemper medicine. It worked every time.

The sulfur he would mix with the pine tar as a worming potion. Out would come the tongue, down would go the stick, swallow, and the horse was wormed.

I have no idea where these remedies came from, and I don't know if Old Al's distrust of the medical profession was based on some experience or because he'd had to make do so much of the time. But he was adamant in the effectiveness of his treatments.

Of all the "drugs" Al used, it was sulfur that he had the most faith in. Perhaps this was because he used it to save his wife and children from the terrible epidemic of Spanish Flu in 1918, when people all over the world were dying and no advances of modern medicine helped them.

The flu appeared toward the end of World War I, and killed over twenty-two million people around the world before it ran its course. In America, half a million died. More Americans died from the Spanish Flu than in any war the country had fought to that time.

And doctors could do nothing, really. The Havre, Montana,

Democrat advised its readers to "Go to Bed and Stay Quiet - Take a Laxative - Eat Plenty of Nourishing Food - Keep Up Your Strength - Nature Is the Only Cure."

But nature wasn't much help. The flu first reached Montana in late September 1918. By the time three months had passed, over 37,000 Montanans had caught it—and the health authorities thought the actual number was twice that, since reporting and record keeping in rural America at such a time of crisis was not the first thing on the mind of the victim or his family. What is known is that over 3,000 Montanans died from Spanish Flu in the first six weeks of the epidemic.

No place was remote enough, not even the wild Canadian valley with Big Bar Creek tumbling through it, there at the edge of the wilderness of the Fraser Plateau. The virus struck there, too, and killed, and there was no remedy and no sanctuary, and enough fear to alter the air in a room with its smell. So Old Al turned to the things he had most faith in, the medicines which had never let him down.

First, he took the windows out of the house to provide good air circulation. Then, twice a day, he burned sulfur on the wood-burning cook stove. If you've never seen sulfur burn, I'll tell you it just smokes like a son-of-a-bitch—you cannot believe how it smokes. The whole house would fill up with smoke, and my mother remembers how they'd cough and have to go outside to breathe.

Old Al said this was fumigating the house. When they'd

all troop back in for supper he'd make them all eat a dab of sulfur on a teaspoon, Grandma and all ten kids, and he'd do it, too. After a few days of this double dose, the sulfur would be coming out the pores in their skin like a yellow skim, and it would sweat out of their bodies at night, yellowing the sheets.

Grandma said it was terrible what that man put them through, but that was just for starters. The clincher was, night after night, he made them eat fat.

My mother told me that for thirty days, while the epidemic was burning through the country and killing people, Old Al made them eat stew loaded with fat. Mom said she could remember the bubbles of fat on top of this stew, floating. If it was beef fat, it wasn't too bad, but if it was back fat off a deer, it was a different story.

Deer fat will stick to the roof of your mouth. Eat some stew with deer fat in it and the fat goes right to the roof of your mouth and sticks there. Fat from beef won't do that, but deer fat will. I don't know why it does, but try some one day and you'll see what I mean. Mom said they'd have to scratch that fat off the roof of their mouths with their fingers. In later years, she was unable to look at a stew.

Even when I was growing up, Old Al still believed in the value of fat. We'd be eating supper, and I start cutting the fat off of my meat and he'd say, "Damn it, eat that, it's good for you!"

So that old man fed his family sulfur and fat-laden stew,

while the Spanish Flu raged around them. When the epidemic was over, none of the Neases had died, none had even fallen sick, and Old Al's faith in sulfur and himself had become further entrenched.

He had survived, and those in his care had survived, without help from doctors, or modern medicine, or anything but his own firm belief in what was right.

Justice and Understanding

Old Al hated a petty thief, somebody who'd steal a chicken or swipe the halter off a man's horse as it leaned over the fence by the county road.

"I admire a man who'll rob a bank," he'd say. "At least he's got guts enough to go after somethin'."

Not that Al advocated robbing banks. It was just that he felt a man should put himself on the line and have some real need if he was gonna break the law. It had to be done for some legitimate purpose. And there had to be risk involved for it to be manly. For example, there was the horse thief Old Al put under the blankets in the bed next to Grandma to hide him from the Mounties.

As horse thieves go this one wasn't much, nor was the horse he'd stolen and sold for twenty dollars. The thief was a fifteen-year-old orphan boy who cleaned out the stables in town for the privilege of sleeping in a room in the barn. The horse was a no-good counterfeit bastard who wasn't worth a damn thing, not even the hay it took to keep his sorry belly full. This kid took him and sold him, and that was wrong under the law, but he was hungry. So now the Canadian Mounted Police were chasing him, and when they caught him he was looking at maybe ten years in jail and the ruination of his life before he'd had a chance to get something going for himself. He was one jump ahead of the Mounties when he pulled into Old Al's place on foot and told him what he'd done.

Could be Old Al saw a little bit of himself in this kid. Al had been on his own since age nine and had to get by however he could, too. He also saw that this was basically a good kid who needed a break if he was gonna to go down the right road in life. If the Mounties got him, he'd be on another path by the time he got out of prison.

Well, these Mounties were right on the kid's tail, so Old Al had Grandma get into bed, and he put the kid under the covers, pressed between her and the wall. When the police came and told him they wanted to search the house, Old Al said, "O.K., but my wife is sick and I don't want her disturbed."

"No, no," said the Mountie in charge. "We won't even go in the bedroom."

So those Mounties searched the house, and they peeked in the bedroom door and saw Grandma lying there with her back to them. There were no closets in the room, and the bed was one of them old-fashioned high ones with the springs way up off the floor so they could see there was nobody under it. They thanked Al and left.

He kept this kid hidden for a couple of days, and then gave him a horse and directions to the place of a friend of his across the border in Montana, where the kid could find a real job to support himself. Grandma told me they got letters from the kid for many years after his brush with the law, and he turned out O.K., so Old Al's idea of right and wrong worked out good that time. He also thought Moses Paul and Paul Spinlin done the right thing when they killed the drummer and put an axe through the Chinaman's head.

Moses Paul and Paul Spinlin were two Indians who lived in the country near Clinton. One night them and their wives met up with a traveling peddler. They had supper together and got to drinking and pretty soon everybody passed out except the drummer. He stole one of the women and took off with her in his wagon.

Eventually, Paul and Spinlin caught up with him, killed him, and took the woman back. But now they were murderers, and the Mounties and a posse of civilians were chasing after them to bring them to justice.

Andrew joined the posse for the adventure and for the good money it paid. But Old Al had nothing to do with it. He felt the drummer had got what was coming for kidnapping the man's wife, and that should have been the end of it, just as he thought the Chinaman got what he deserved.

Moses Paul and Paul Spinlin evaded the posse for many months, largely because just about every Indian in the territory and many whites were helping them. In particular, there was this one Chinaman who they say kept them supplied. He lived in a dugout, and had arranged for Paul and Spinlin to come there one night to get another load of stuff. Cautious as always, they sneaked up on the place real careful, each from opposite directions, and what they found was a whole bunch of Mounted Police lying in ambush. The Chinaman had been tempted by the reward, which by now was substantial.

Paul and Spinlin slipped away, but they returned the next night. Spinlin climbed up on the roof of the dugout and crouched over the door with a double-bladed ax in his hands. Paul called to the Chinaman, and when he stepped through the door to see who was there, Spinlin put the ax through his face in return for his treachery.

Old Al thought that was simple justice.

Meanwhile, Paul and Spinlin were tearing through the country ahead of the authorities and their posse, who couldn't seem to catch them. They were good runners, and bold, too. One night, they even crawled into the posse's camp and stole a bunch of things while their pursuers slept, including the pair of field glasses Andrew had borrowed from Old Al.

One day Grandma was driving along the road in her buggy

when Paul and Spinlin went by with their horses at a dead run. Spinlin had one white eye, and as they raced past, he turned toward Grandma and looked at her hard. She was pregnant at the time, and for the months before it was born she feared the outlaw had "marked her baby" with his stare.

Another day, the two came upon Howard as he was holding a herd of horses in a meadow. They were chasing a big black gelding who ran into the bunch. Paul approached Howard and asked, "You help me catch that horse?" Howard looked over his shoulder and saw Spinlin pointing a .30-.30 at him, and he said, "Sure! I'll help you!"

There are two versions of how they eventually got caught. One is that another Indian betrayed them for the reward. Grandma always said it was a Catholic priest who talked them into giving themselves up. Either way, Spinlin got himself hung, and Paul went to jail, where he was killed. Grandma says Spinlin's mother went high up on a mountain and danced and wailed with her arms raised high and put a curse on the jury, whose members began dying one by one of causes that weren't natural. Old Al thought that was justice, too.

Old Al was on the receiving end of a more subtle kind of justice for his own sins, most often at the hands of Grandma, who had her own sense of right and wrong.

Old Al never did shake loose of his love of drinking, and would go off from time to time on bouts with his buddies that lasted for days. One of the memorable ones occurred in the dead of a bad winter, and while he was gone the temperature dropped suddenly and the snow started falling. The homestead was a good thirty-five miles from town, so Grandma and the kids were stuck good. So was Al, wherever he was, but that didn't matter to him. If anything, it gave the bunch an excuse to stay put and keep drinking.

But Grandma had to keep the home place going, with ten kids and all. Fortunately, they had plenty of beef and garden produce put up, but firewood was another matter. They ran out soon enough, and with the wind howling at the door, she would have to go out into the storm and split up some more. But Grandma looked out in the barnyard and saw Al's new pig feeder.

This was one mighty fine new wooden rack for feeding hogs, which Al had made that summer from new boards hauled by wagon from Clinton. He was real proud of that pig feeder. It made his own chores a lot easier to handle, and was an important part of his pig operation.

In the spring, Al and his neighbors ferried all their hogs across the Fraser River and drove them for six days into a part of the woods where wild potatoes grew, and the pigs rooted them out and fed on them all summer. In the fall, the pigs would march out of the woods on their own, swim the river, and come home.

"There goes Al's old sow," one neighbor would say every fall as the hogs paraded up the road. "Must be gettin' cold soon."

Over the winter, Al would feed them grain he'd grown, in his wooden pig feeder. It was his masterpiece, put together with great labor and expense. But as Grandma looked out across the drifting snow, what she saw was the easiest solution to the problem of keeping her and the kids warm.

When the storm broke and Al finally come home, she had new pine boards stacked to the ceiling by the stove, which was glowing warmly. "Well," said Old Al, "I knew you'd handle it. But Goddamn, I wish you hadn't cut up them pig feeders."

A man or a woman cannot have a sense of justice without having understanding and the ability to forgive, too. Perhaps it comes from experience. The more mistakes a person makes, the more his tolerance for the shortcomings of others. In any event, the capacity of Old Al and Grandma to understand and forgive was tested in 1926, when Grandma decided it was time to move away from the homestead on the banks of Big Bar Creek. What led to that decision was Violet's marriage to an Indian.

Violet was the second daughter of the seven girls in the family, and she had given in to the isolation and the shortage of eligible men and had become pregnant by a young Shuswap, which led to the marriage which Grandma never would have otherwise permitted.

"East is east and west is west," she'd say, "and never the twain shall meet." She was talking about mixing the races here, and she drew on her Bible as the authority for her stern views. There were six other Neas girls yet unmarried, and she was determined that they would not marry Indians. So she told Al it was time to move back to civilization.

When they had met over twenty-five years earlier, he had told her, "There's this valley in Montana that's the prettiest place that ever was." And that is where he had decided, after his allotted years of roaming and chasing gold had passed, to make his final stand. He was talking about the Flathead Valley, south of Glacier Park, touching the great Flathead Lake, a place of greenness and mountains and opportunity, still.

It's no surprise that Al remembered the Flathead country. He had seen it in its pristine beauty in 1879, and it remains today a lovely place, though filling up with outsiders at a frightful rate.

In 1890, a little promotional booklet called "Flathead Facts" told readers,

> It must be seen to be appreciated and all manner of description can not do [it] justice. The visitor . . . is astonished at its magnitude and leaves the country so favorably impressed that he at once contemplates returning to it and investing in its landed wealth.

So it was with Old Al, who was once again willing to move when his wife insisted, but this time he did it with the feeling that he was going home, and that the struggles of his working life were mostly behind him.

By now, his holdings in British Columbia had grown to comfortable proportions. Al had his homestead along Big Bar Creek and his wheat land on the mountain. He ran cattle on the open range around the Fraser, and a man who knew the family well, Henry Grinder, says there were never fewer than two hundred horses with Old Al's brand on them. By any measure in those times, in that place, he was a success, confident in himself and secure.

But Al had never been to school and could neither read nor write. His younger brother Andrew had gone through the sixth or seventh grade, though, so Al dispatched him to the Flathead Valley to make a trade for all Al owned in British Columbia for something of equal value there. It was a plan that should have set them up for life if Andrew had not had his own weakness for liquor.

By the time Andrew returned to the homestead on Big Bar Creek, he had gotten drunk in Kalispell and traded everything for a one-bedroom house on 160 acres, mostly brush—rough, dry brush land that couldn't be tilled. After one night of Andrew's drinking, all Old Al had worked for to provide for himself and his wife and his ten kids was virtually gone. Gone were the cattle and most of the horses and the house on the creek and the wheat lands and the machinery. In their place was a house too small for the family to move into, and land too poor to farm. Gone with the contents of the bottle was all Al had built in the past and what he had saved for the future.

What could he do? There was nothing he could do but press on. So Al loaded his furniture and his family onto two wagons, one of them to be driven by Grandma. He had saved about fifty of his horses from the deal, and these he would drive himself, with some help from Howard. But before they pulled away from Big Bar Creek, Old Al was subjected to one final indignity.

He butchered a two-year-old heifer from the place and Grandma canned the meat for the trip. About that time, the man the new owners sent up to keep an eye on things arrived and accused Al of stealing the cow. Al insisted that the owners had allowed him that one heifer. But the Mounties wouldn't let him leave until the matter was cleared up. So for a week, Al held his horses and his wagons and his family on a meadow outside of town while word was sent to Montana and back again, and sure enough, Old Al had got permission to butcher the animal, so they were finally on their way.

As they approached the border, Al realized he had another problem. He didn't have money to pay the duty on his horses, and he sure as hell wasn't about to leave them behind. The customs regulations said that in addition to what pulled your wagon, you were allowed one extra team. So Al put harnesses on a mighty fine pair of Thoroughbred mares he really liked and tied them behind Grandma's wagon.

"They won't believe they're a spare team," she protested, and it was a bit of a long shot. The mares were fine-boned and dainty, real pretty horses, and obviously not wagon-pullers.

"Just do it," said Old Al.

As for the other horses, his plan was to slip them across the border himself—swim them across the Columbia River alone—and thus avoid the customs officers and the duty he couldn't pay.

So they separated, and Grandma and the kids did what Old Al said, and sure enough, the wagons made it through the customs station without a bit of trouble. Of Old Al they saw nothing. Some time later as they headed down the road a car pulled up and the driver leaned out. "Are you Mrs. Neas?" he asked.

"Sure am," replied Grandma.

"Well, I passed an old man with white hair and a bunch of horses some ways back," the man continued. "He says for you to find a good place to camp and he'll be along."

And two days later, he was.

They were three months on the road, Old Al and his horses and Grandma and the two wagons with all their possessions in them, and all the kids except Violet, who'd stayed behind with her Shuswap Indian husband. For the younger kids, the days were full of discovery. When young Daisy saw her first telephone lines she said, "Wow! They sure hang their clothes high in this country!" And the first time she saw a water wagon wetting down the dirt road she declared, "He'll lose all his water before he gets it home!"

But I've often wondered what went through the mind of Old Al as he rode down the road in the dust of the wagons and the horse herd. He was coming on sixty years old, and was faced with starting over again. The Great Depression was about to begin, and whatever cushion he had built to weather such times was now gone. But in all the years I lived with him while I grew up, I never once heard him mention what Andrew had done by way of explaining the poor way we lived, and I never once heard him complain.

Grandma was a different story. I remember one time when I was young and we was all sitting around the kitchen table at our rented place near Kila. Andrew, who continued to live with them, was complaining about how every cent he made went into the family pot to help keep the place afloat. He went on and on about this for a while, and then Grandma turned away from her wood-burning cook stove and looked at him hard.

She never cursed and disapproved of others doing it, but this time she pointed her wooded spoon at Andrew and said, "And I appreciate what you're doin'! But don't you ever forget, you son-of-a-bitch, you're the one who broke us! You and your damn whiskey!"

Old Al just sat there, saying nothing.

The Blind Pigs

The Flathead Valley country was about to get clobbered by the Great Depression around the time Old Al moved his family in, but folks there had already figured out how to deal with another troublesome condition: Prohibition. They had a saying around Kalispell back then, "Prohibition is better than no whiskey at all."

Jerry March ran the Rainbow Texaco station in Kalispell for many years, and he remembers when he was a little kid living in Scobey in the '20s he'd sometimes hear a knock on the door of their farmhouse real late at night, and he knew what that meant.

It meant his dad would get up and hitch up the team and go to pull some bootlegger out of the mud. Their farm was only about twelve miles from the Canadian border, and the bootleggers would make their runs at night. The problem was, they had what they called "gumbo roads" up there, and after a rain the roads would just turn to thick, clinging mud you couldn't drive through very well. So Jerry's dad got called out frequently. In the morning after such a job, there'd be a case of beer or two or three bottles of whiskey on the porch, left there as payment for the favor.

And Jerry remembers his mother visiting her friend on the next farm, an otherwise law-abiding lady who that day was boiling bootleg whiskey on the stove, adding charred oak chips to it to give it that aged flavor. Her family supplemented its farm income by selling moonshine at the Wolf Point Stampede.

Prohibition worked in Montana about as well as it worked anywhere. Phil Johnson was a young man driving a bread truck in those days, and he says he once figured there were twenty-three places in and around Kalispell where a man could get a drink. One old moonshiner said the number was twice that. If true, there were more places to get illegal whiskey in Kalispell during Prohibition than there are licensed bars there today.

Charlie MacDonald, a part-Nez Perce Indian related to Chief Joseph, cowboyed and packed some with Old Al. He says you could ride out of Niarada a couple of miles in any direction and come upon a still. You'd be going along past some old deserted farm in the early morning, and pretty soon smoke would start coming out of the chimney—and they weren't cooking eggs for breakfast.

They say the man who was to become my father, Mark Hall, ran a still near Libby. He was working it one day when the sheriff came out to warn him that federal agents were in the area sniffing around, and he suggested that Mark shut things down for a while. My future dad didn't pay any attention to the warning, though, and the Feds caught him. A judge invited him to be a guest in the prison on McNeil Island in Washington for thirteen months.

Apparently it wasn't unusual for some of the local law to be on the inside of things. One old moonshiner said the price he had to pay to buy a cop was a half a deer and a gallon of whiskey a month, and often he had to poach the deer. One real good way to get caught, he said, was for a moonshiner to give whiskey away to his neighbors. Sometimes in those days all a man could make doing honest labor was a dollar a day, and the neighbors who were working honest would be jealous of the man making more money selling whiskey and they'd turn him in.

When that happened, "They'd send you to school for ninety days," he said. Meaning you'd cool your heels in some jail for three months.

The moonshine makers went to some lengths to avoid being noticed, like they wouldn't buy all their sugar in one place. And they knew the authorities could locate a still in town by monitoring the amount of water and electricity a person used. So they came up with ways to hide their activities.

A man who made a lot of moonshine back then says they'd attach a magnet to the outside of the water meter to make the wheel inside stop turning. Then it wouldn't record the true amount of water they were using. They'd remove the magnet just before the meter reader showed up.

And they'd transport their whiskey in "mixed loads," that is, wagons or trucks loaded with hay, or wood, or vegetables, or "whatever it took to make you look like a workin' man."

There was good enough money in the enterprise if a guy could keep from getting caught. The whiskey run into Kalispell from Canada sold for as much as ten dollars a quart. The booze made in town would sell for something like four dollars a gallon. Why the difference? The cost of doing business—real and potential—was much higher on the Canadian run.

"You had to take a chance on your life, your wagon, and all your belongings," said the old moonshiner. "The Feds would confiscate everything if they caught you."

And maybe there was then, as now, something attractive about imported products.

A man could make moonshine for about a dollar a gallon, so the potential profits where high, despite the risks. A good moonshiner could make as much as two hundred gallons of booze a month, but not everyone had enough capital to finance an operation that big.

It's been over fifty years since the old moonshiner has

brewed up a batch, but when asked about the recipe he remembered it with the sureness of a man who had used it many times.

"You start with a fifty-gallon barrel," he recalled.

"You mean a metal drum?"

"Hell no! You don't use no metal at all! One nail will cut the alcohol content twenty percent!"

"O.K., a wooden barrel."

"Right. You dump in water that's not too hot. Add one hundred pounds of sugar, and one pound of Fleischmann's yeast."

"What kind of yeast?"

"Fleischmann's yeast. The kind you get from the bakery."

"O.K."

"Then dump in one-half gallon of molasses to keep it from foamin' over. Then stir.

"Now you let it sit. How long depends on the weather and how hot it is. If you're doin' this upstairs in the summer with a window over the barrel, it might have to sit three days."

"What do you mean, a 'window over the barrel'?"

"You know, a piece of glass. You cover the barrel with a window. Then it might be ready in three days. But usually, it takes five."

"How do you know when it's ready?"

"Well, you hold a match over the barrel, and when it don't put the match out, it's ready."

"What puts the match out? Fumes?"

"Yeah. It sends up little geysers. Anyway, when it don't put the match out, it's ready to run.

"You need a sixty-gallon still to run it in so it don't boil over. You dump your fifty gallons in there and get it to boilin' good. The steam comes up and goes through fifty feet of three-quarter-inch copper tube in a thirty-gallon barrel. That cooled it."

"Where would you get all this copper tubing?"

"I got mine from 'The Copper Can Kid' in Whitefish. By God, when he cemented somethin' together with solder, it stayed there!"

"So you cooled these tubes with water?"

"Right. In the winter we used snow. That would make the alcohol condense out of the steam."

"How potent would it be?"

"The first bit to come out of the still would be over a hundred proof. Toward the end of the run, it would be down to thirty proof."

"How did you know?"

"Measured it with a hydrometer. What you sold had to be at least eighty proof if you wanted to keep your reputation up."

"How much would you get?"

"From a hundred pounds of sugar, you'd get about ten gallons of whiskey. But the main thing is, when the first quart or so comes out, use it for startin' fires."

"Why's that?"

"It's got all the copper rust in it out of the pipes."

"What would happen if you drank it?"

"It could make you go blind."

They say a lot of people in Kalispell made a lot of money off of whiskey during Prohibition—making it and running it—and they can name affluent families and prominent businesses in town they say got to where they are today with the help of money from moonshine.

The houses in town where you could go to get a drink were known as "Blind Pigs." Nobody wants to mention names of people who ran them even though all this happened a long time ago, but they still like to tell stories, leaving out their own names, too, of course.

One man who lives in Kalispell today remembers the day he and a buddy went to have a drink at a local "Blind Pig." On their way up to the house, they noticed a large pile of broken glass on the lawn of the back yard, sure evidence that the Feds had raided the place recently, and busted things up. They knocked on the door and asked the lady of the house what had happened.

"Well," she said, "I had visitors, but come in anyway. Drinks are on the house."

"What do you mean, 'drinks are on the house?'" the man asked. "You just got busted."

The woman led them into the front hall. She kicked a button at the bottom of the banister post, releasing a hidden spring hinge. The top of the post flew open. She reached down inside the hollow post and pulled out a gallon jug of whiskey the Feds had missed and poured the drinks.

The federal agents also missed a chance when they raided the house of a moonshiner near Kila. His wife was the only one home at the time, and she was washing clothes in an old-fashioned washtub when the telltale knocks came at the front and back doors simultaneously. Fortunately for her, the only bootleg whiskey in the house at the time was one jug, which she hurriedly poked down into the tub under the clothes.

While the agents searched the place, the heat from the wash water started up some kind of reaction in the jug that caused gas to form and pop the cork. Fumes of warm whiskey filled the house, but the Feds never found the source and left frustrated.

But they scored often enough to make moonshining a risky business, and not everyone who engaged in it got rich. Some were lucky to make a living at it, and many got caught and were punished. But even so, old-timers in Kalispell can't resist a smile when they remember those years.

There's the story of one moonshiner who was sent before the judge and got convicted.

"I fine you two hundred and fifty dollars," was the sentence from the bench.

"Why sure, Judge," said the offender cheerfully. "I got it right here in my back pocket!" And he hauled out some of his profits.

"And I sentence you to six months in jail!" replied the enraged judge. "You got that in your back pocket, too?"

One well-known moonshiner was Dan "Dogie" Duncan. In the spring of 1926 he was charged with possessing intoxicating liquor. When the county sheriff and a couple of city police went to arrest him, they found him not at home. They went on in anyway, seized some evidence, and arrested Dogie when he returned.

His lawyer argued that the authorities had no right to enter the house and take anything because all they had was an arrest warrant, not a search warrant, and he moved that the evidence they had gathered be suppressed. The judge agreed. Dogie then asked that his property be returned. The judge agreed to that, too.

So that judge ordered Flathead County Sheriff J. O. Morton to return "two paper bags full of corks, one box of bottle caps, three 12-gallon stone jars, one 15-gallon stone jar, seventy empty whiskey flasks, pints and half pints, one-hundred-and-forty-seven empty quart beer bottles, and six barrels of empty beer bottles."

Dogie Duncan then pleaded not guilty to the charge of possession of liquor.

The judge sentenced him to ninety days in the county jail anyway.

So, a good many citizens in Kalispell and the surrounding area certainly winked at the Prohibition laws, if they didn't actively violate them, and into this environment came the Neas family, Old Al and Ruth Ella and the nine kids still with them, looking for an opportunity to start over.

When they arrived, the citizens of Kalispell were not only preoccupied with Prohibition and how to get around it, they also seemed mighty interested in crime in general, maybe even fascinated by it. And they still were four years later, if you can judge by what the local daily newspaper figured its readers wanted.

Take the front page of *The Daily Inter Lake* for August 18, 1930, for example. Of twenty-two front-page stories, ten were about violence and death, including such far-away incidents as "New York Jobless Trample Aged Man In Rush For Work," "Tragedy Stalks Oregon Highways," and "Californians Die As Auto Plunges."

Inside was an editorial on how the mayor of Toronto, World War I flying ace Bert Wemp, kept a lid on crime in his city. (One of his main points was "because we control the liquor situation.") And the paper's serialized novel was titled *Murder At High Tide.*

But the news story from that day in 1930 that people talked about most and still talk about today changed the Neas family forever. The banner headline in big, black type all across the top of page one announced:

"TWO KILLED IN GUN FIGHT NEAR KILA"

Butterflies and Blood

Funny, isn't it, how people remember the smallest things about the most important days?

Austin Monk, now in his eighties, remembers a great deal about August 17, 1930, the day Dogie Duncan killed my Uncle Budd. Austin saw his friend Budd lying in the dust of a country road, soaking in a pool of his own blood.

Nearby was Russell Austin, lying on his stomach, propping himself up with his elbows, head hanging, a bullet in his back. Across the road lay Gus Austin, his head beaten, dry grass sticking to his bloody whiskers, such a mess of blood and whiskers and hair and grass that you couldn't tell if he was face up or face down. Every once in a while, he'd kick and flop over.

Austin Monk took all this in, and still he remembers, very clearly, the robin sitting on the fence post there, singing its heart out, as if the best thing in the whole wide world to be on that day was a bird in the sunshine of summer, with plenty of worms to eat and not a thought yet of the winter to come.

Austin Monk also remembers driving up that country road minutes earlier in his Model "A" Ford coupe with his girlfriend and another couple to meet his pal Budd, as they'd arranged just a short time before. Suddenly this frantic woman jumped out in front of him.

"I was probably drivin' thirty-five miles an hour down that gravel road," he recalls clearly to this day. "She jumped right out in front of me and waved her hands and I stepped on the brakes. That turned it the other way, you know, and she jumped out on the other side of me and waved. I couldn't hardly keep from hittin' her. Every way I turned the car, she was jumpin' in front of me, tryin' to get me to stop."

It was Ruth Ella Neas. She'd heard the shots, and then somebody'd come to the house and told her Budd was hurt, and she'd started running up the road along Smith Lake toward the sound of the guns. Austin Monk picked her up, and a little further on lay Budd, dead in the dust and the blood.

Today, you can find people here and there around Kalispell who think Budd and the Austins had it coming. And you'll find many others who think Dogie Duncan got off too easy, spending just a bit over twelve years of his life sentence for murder in the state prison at Deer Lodge.

But it's very, very hard to find a person who doesn't think this was a really stupid crime that never should have happened, and probably wouldn't have if it hadn't been for moonshine whiskey and bad judgment. In the end, it cost three lives and ruined another.

It started with an argument over who owned a cowhide robe worth maybe three dollars.

The details of what happened during that summer Sunday vary depending on who you believe. But one way or another, the participants in the tragedy came together that afternoon at the Stopher place on the west side of Smith Lake in a little valley west of Kalispell.

There was Gus Austin, a traveling salesman for a Salt Lake City clothing company. He maintained the cowhide robe was his, given to him by Dogie Duncan's father, Dan.

There was Russell Austin, Gus's nephew, who operated the steam engine in the Somers lumberyard. He was up to visit his mother, and had brought with him his wife and four-month-old baby.

There was Dogie Duncan, known widely around the county as a moonshiner. He had been fined and jailed for violating the Prohibition laws, and charged several other times. Dogie was forty-two years old, divorced, the father of four. That morning he had visited his children, taking them watermelon and cookies. He disputed Gus Austin's claim to the cowhide robe.

There was Wilbur Uttley, eighteen years old, Dogie's nephew. And there was Budd.

Budd Burnett Neas, age nineteen, was Ruth Ella's favorite child, it seemed, and he was always very good to her. He wasn't the cowhand that his brother Howard and his father Old Al were, but he could ride and often did. He could train a horse to do anything he wanted, to bow, or count with its hooves, all those fancy tricks.

There were differing opinions about Budd's personality around Kalispell back then, and there still are today. You can hear, for example, that he was a bully who'd go out of his way to pick a fight, and then would be brutal once it started. You'll hear, too, that he was a peaceful young man, never looked for trouble, but a young man who possessed that strong Neas trait that didn't allow anyone to push him.

So there they were that Sunday afternoon, hanging around the Stopher place with some other people. Budd and Wilbur Uttley had attended a dance in Holt the night before with Austin Monk, stopped at Stopher's at 7 A.M., gone on to Kalispell for breakfast, visited various people, and wound up back at Stopher's late in the morning. And moonshine liquor played a major role in what happened that day.

A man named Walter Torbenson said he had a couple of drinks with Budd and Wilbur before nine that morning. Mrs. Cassius Duncan said the two young men were drunk before that. Others say they'd been drinking on and off, but weren't intoxicated. John Hoyt said they were so drunk before noon he had to help them out of Austin Monk's car at Stopher's and dump them in a garage to sleep it off. But Monk says this isn't so.

In any event, there was no shortage of booze that day, Prohibition aside. Dogie Duncan passed a pint around when he joined the crowd at Stopher's, and at one point got into a row with Wilbur Uttley over some whiskey he thought Wilbur had stolen. Jim Austin said he even heard Dogie threatened to kill Wilbur over the supposed theft.

Things were rolling along when Gus Austin arrived in his Ford touring car. A woman named Barbara Shaw said she'd seen him a short time earlier, drunk, and saying he was going to "get even with that Duncan outfit." What he meant is unclear, but with the arrival of Gus Austin the scene was set, because he had with him the cowhide robe, which he used to keep his passengers warm.

Dogie Duncan told Gus his father wanted the robe back, and that he'd just take it then and there. Gus refused to hand it over, insisting angrily that the elder Duncan had given it to him to keep. To settle the matter, Dogie proposed they put the question to his father, who lived just a quarter mile down the road.

At that point, Austin Monk was ready to leave, and asked Budd to come with him and his girlfriend on a ride up to Truman Creek.

"We'll be back in just half an hour or forty-five minutes," Monk said.

"No, you go ahead," replied Budd, hanging his suit coat on the gate of the picket fence. "I want to go along and see how this argument comes out. Pick me up when you come back."

Also interested in the outcome of the quarrel were Russell Austin, Gus's nephew, and Wilbur Uttley. So they all piled into the touring car along with the cowhide robe, and off they went.

Dan Duncan was feeding his hogs when the party arrived. Dogie asked him if he'd given the robe to Gus Austin. Dan said, no, he hadn't, that in fact, he wanted Dogie to have it.

Dogie said in that case he'd just go get it out of the car.

"No you won't," said Gus, and the fight was on.

At this point, Dogie and his father tell one version of the fight, Wilbur Uttley a different one. The Duncans say Budd and Russell Austin both jumped Dogie, that Budd hit him on the head with something hard and knocked him down.

"From then on, I was on the ground," Dogie testified in court later. "Russell and Budd were both fighting me, and every time I tried to get up, one of them would pull me down. Finally, one of them kicked me in the stomach."

The senior Duncan testified that it was Budd who kicked Dogie, and that the fight ended with Russell Austin beating Dogie over the head with a rock.

Wilbur Uttley told the court the fight was between Dogie and Russell, and that Budd's only contribution was to tell

Dogie to "Get up and fight like a man." Wilbur said further that Dogie got the wound to his head when it hit the rock foundation of the house.

However it happened, things could have ended right there with Dogie lying on the ground stunned and the fight over. Dan Duncan ordered the men off his property, helped his son into the house, and went to his garage for some liniment. Budd and the others returned to the car and got ready to leave.

Then suddenly, Dogie came back out of the house. He had with him a .32-caliber Winchester rifle.

"I went down to the car and said 'I'm going to take the robe,'" he testified in court. "Budd grinned at me and said he'd shove the rifle up my ass and stooped to pick up a rock. Then I shot at Budd and Russell, and as Gus came at me, I hit him with the gun and broke it. As he charged me again, I hit him with the barrel."

A stunned Wilbur Uttley was the only one to escape. "I looked up and saw Dogie comin'," he said in court. "He fired and Budd dropped. I ran across the road and into a field, and when I stopped, I saw Dogie running Russell and Gus around the car. I heard a shot and saw Russell drop.

"I ran again and stopped when I saw Dogie hit Gus with his fist or the gun, I don't know which. Then I saw him swing the rifle and knock Gus down."

Dan Duncan ran out of the garage when he heard the

shots and met his son returning to the house with the rifle barrel in his hands. "Dad, I've stood all I could," he said. "I guess I've killed those fellows." And then he drove off to get the sheriff.

Wilbur Uttley continued running across the fields until he came to the Stopher place, where he told them what had happened. He then ran on to give the news to Ruth Ella, Al being away at the time, working over in Niarada.

So after a day of moonshine whiskey and an argument over a cowhide robe, Budd Neas lay dead.

Russell Austin died in the Kalispell hospital later that night. Gus Austin hung on for several weeks in a hospital in Salt Lake City, then he died from the injuries he'd received when Dogie broke the rifle over his head. Dogie Duncan was charged with murder in the second degree.

His defense attorneys attempted to get him off in a couple of ways. First, they tried to show that he couldn't get a fair trial in Kalispell for two reasons: pre-trial publicity and his own reputation.

They got depositions from a variety of people, including Albert Dreesen, who was part owner of a store called "The Palm" in Kalispell, where he sold cigars, candy, and soft drinks. He swore that people talked about the case all the time in his store and had firm opinions about the guilt or innocence of Dogie Duncan and the punishment he should receive. Dreesen also said that his customers felt, regardless of the facts of this case, that Dogie should be punished for repeatedly violating the liquor laws.

And the defense attorneys got a deposition from Kalispell druggist J. H. C. Fitch, who felt that the case was so well known that they'd have trouble seating a jury. Fitch felt that they'd have to call a large number of prospective jurors and a large number of them would be disqualified, "all of which would entail great and unusual expense upon the taxpayers."

Duncan's attorney Hans Walchli said that the coroner's inquest, reported in detail by the press, had developed only the state's side of the case, and presented a distorted and one-sided picture of what had happened. The large headline in the *Kalispell News*, for example, screamed "Dogie Duncan Runs Amuck."

On its side, the prosecution brought out John Welden, a traveling insurance salesman, who allowed as how he'd heard some discussion of the case, but none that would indicate that the people of Flathead County were inflamed against Duncan. A traveling salesman for the Kalispell Mercantile agreed. And so did Ralph Ripke, the sheriff of Flathead County, who said he'd heard some casual references to the case, but not much expressions of opinion about guilt or innocence.

Dogie Duncan was tried in Kalispell in early December 1930. His plea was self-defense. His lawyers attempted to prove that he had been so badly beaten that he had been temporarily deranged. Their expert witness, Dr. H. J. Bailey, testified that Duncan could have acted under an irresistible impulse, that it was possible for him to have acted in self-defense without thinking rationally.

Prosecutor Child then approached Dr. Bailey. "You have testified," he said, "to the injuries in medical terms, but in ordinary language, you mean that the defendant had a black eye, a cut on the forehead, and a bruise on the stomach which might have been caused by an ordinary blow."

The medical arguments continued until early afternoon of December 9th. The jury got the case the next day, and by seven that night it had convicted Dogie Duncan of second-degree murder. Judge Pomeroy sentenced him to life in prison.

Dogie almost made it out of Deer Lodge State Prison some eleven years later when Governor Ford commuted his sentence. But the Board of Pardons overturned the governor. The clerk of the board commented in a letter to a member of Dogie's family that "the volume of correspondence from Flathead County was such that the board could not ignore it." It was the weight of these letters, said the clerk, plus the fact that Dogie Duncan had murdered three men, that caused the board to refuse to agree to the governor's recommendation.

But a year later the board changed its mind, and Dogie was released from prison in July 1943. He moved to San Francisco and worked in the shipyards there.

And Austin Monk still remembers the small things about

the day his friend Budd died. He remembers Ruth Ella sitting in the dirt of the road, cradling her dead son's head in her lap. He remembers how neatly Budd was dressed and how clean his shirt was. Ruth Ella undid his tie and unbuttoned his shirt, looking for his wound. And Austin Monk said she cursed the man who'd killed him as thoroughly as he's ever heard a man cursed, and she didn't use one cuss word.

Ruby, Russell Austin's young wife, remembers to this day how lovely the sunset was that evening. And she remembers Ruth Ella singing as she held Budd. The song was "Nearer My God to Thee."

Ruth Ella remembered the small things, too. In later years she would tell about the white butterfly that flittered down as she sat there in the road with Budd's head in her lap, the butterfly that landed in the pool of his blood and fluttered about for a while. When it flew off, its white wings were stained with red.

The Bronc Rider

I was just shy of fifteen years old when I walked in on Grandma and told her I wanted to quit school. All a person had to do to meet the law in those days was go to school until you were sixteen or complete the eighth grade, whichever came first. I'd completed the eighth grade and figured if that was good enough for the law, it was sure good enough for me.

I'd hated school from the first day Grandma made me go, and I hated it right up to the end. I suffered my way through the first eight grades at the little Kila school, more interested in playing softball at recess than anything else, and then came the big turning point. To go to high school, I had to ride the bus to Kalispell. I sat through classes all the first week, went back to give 'er another go the following Monday, and then I figured that was about all it was worth. It was boring, and I didn't have no money, and couldn't earn none while I was sitting in some dumb classroom. I wanted to be a cowboy, and they sure weren't teaching me anything about that.

But that old lady sure raised hell when I broke her the news.

So I went out to the corrals to see Old Al. He listened to me like always, and when I'd finished, he said, "Well there's no sense in goin' if you're not gonna do somethin'. But you're not gonna lay on your ass around here. You're gonna work."

That was just fine with me. In fact, it was exactly what I had in mind. So I stacked hay in the summer and rode horses for my Uncle Howard, who made a lot of his money breaking horses for folks. He'd give me the easier ones and have me put miles on them for a month, and for that he'd give me fifteen bucks. For a kid with no money in his pocket, fifteen bucks for a month's work was great.

But most of all during that time after I quit school, I wanted to be a rodeo cowboy. God, there was glory in it, and all that attention. I grew up on stories of Charlie Van Cleeve, and Bud and Bill Linderman, and Tommy Three Persons, a great bronc rider Al had known in Canada. There was even two women bronc riders in those days, Marge and Alice Greenough, although they just rode in exhibitions. They weren't allowed to compete against the men. And then, of course, there was my Uncle Howard.

One time a couple of years earlier, Howard had rode this horse he was breaking over to our house from his place, just putting miles on her. This was a real rotten, spoiled bitch that had bucked everybody else off, so the owner was paying Howard to ride her down. After dinner, he went out to the barn to get her for the ride back, and I and Old Al were with him.

Howard got on this horse and she immediately started tossing her head, wanting to buck, but Howard had her on a real tight rein and she couldn't get her head down so she couldn't buck good. Nearby, Grandma was out on the porch, sweeping.

"Why don't you give her her head," said Old Al. "Your ma's watchin.'"

So Howard let that horse go, and she went to bucking. She bucked all around the barnyard, twisting and jumping and thrashing around, but he stayed on top, and when she finally got wore out and quit, Grandma called down from the porch, "Very good, son."

By God, that turned me on. The bucking and the riding and the compliment from Grandma, all of it just seemed to be just the right package, and I wanted to be a bronc rider more than ever. So after I quit school at age fourteen I went to Kalispell to see ol' Burl Drollinger.

Drollinger was an old packer who had some horses that bucked and an arena with some chutes, and he'd help the local boys get started right, so I went down there to get him to teach me how to ride broncs, because I was gonna be a rodeo cowboy for sure.

Old Al did not approve of this venture. He liked good riding and he liked horses that bucked and he liked having his fun at the celebrations after the work was done. But he in no way wanted me to try being a professional rodeo rider because he knew the odds of my ever making a living at it were real slim. It's just like the odds of a kid today growing up to be a pro quarterback. There are damn few of them, and Old Al knew that the real future for me was on a ranch, even if I couldn't see it at the time.

No, I just couldn't see it at all. All I saw down the road was me coming busting out of the chute with one hand high in the air, a horse bowed up under me, dirt a-flyin', and the crowd going wild. They sure didn't teach you about *that* in the ninth grade in Kalispell. So off I went to a better school at Burl Drollinger's arena.

And I tried hard. I really worked at this, but every time I got on a horse, I got my face driven into the dirt. Ol' Burl would be there on the gate a-talking to me and giving me all kind of advice, then the gate would fly open and Bam! Bam! Whop! and I'd be picking myself up again before I'd even got started.

I was so frustrated. It seemed like I never really got settled on the horse's back before the gate opened, and two seconds later, I was in the dirt. You've seen bronc riders at rodeos. They get all set and then they nod to the gate man to turn 'er loose. It just seemed that I never got that far. Things all happened so fast, and before I knew it I was bucked off. One time it even seemed as if the gate opened while Burl was in the middle of a sentence telling me to be sure to have my heels high up on the horse's shoulders as I came out. I was listening real close to him, and suddenly, Bam! Bam! Whop!

One day a horse bucked me off real bad. I went skidding along the ground with the wind knocked out of me, sliding along on my face with my mouth open. I ended up under the gate at the end of the arena with my mouth and nose full of horseshit and sand, spitting and gasping for breath.

That was my last bronc ride and the end of my dream of being a rodeo cowboy. I figured I didn't have the reflexes or something. Once I climbed up on the horse's back, things just happened too fast for me to deal with. I decided right then that I simply hurt too much to go on. It just wasn't worth it. So I walked away from Burl Drollinger's arena, walked away from school for the second time, and headed back to Kila and the ranch and Old Al.

But now that I wasn't gonna get rich as a professional rodeo rider, I was faced with doing something else for what money I needed. Summers were generally O.K., with hay to stack and ranch work available, but winters were a problem until my pal Henry Vlasak and I discovered that there was a good market in Kalispell for poached deer.

Vlasak had followed my example and dropped out of school

a month after I did, and as time went on, he found himself in the same economic bind as me. Then we found that there were people in town who were willing to pay five dollars for a deer. This was a real opportunity. All we'd have to do was shoot it, gut it, and deliver it, hair and all. This was highly illegal, of course, but if people were willing to pay for something ol' Hank and I could deliver, well hell, we were hardly in a position to turn away from it.

So we'd take orders for deer from folks in Kalispell and go up in the hills beyond Kila to fill them at night. In those days there were deer all over the place, great herds of them sometimes, and we never had a problem killing what we needed. The job was made easier by the fact that we used a spotlight to blind the deer and freeze it into immobility before we shot it at close range. We shot bucks, does, anything that had hair on it. Not real sporting, but this was business, not sport, and the people wanted meat and we wanted their money.

One of us would drive the pickup along the mountain road until we saw a deer. Then he'd shine the spotlight in its eyes and the other guy would hop out and shoot it. We'd gut it, throw it in the back of the pickup, flip the tarp over it, and be off. Sometimes we'd fill our orders in less than an hour. This was a real efficient business, usually, but there were occasional glitches, like the time we took Ernie Greg along.

The way we'd set things up that night, Ernie was driving,

I was on the spotlight, and Vlasak was doing the shooting. Ernie was real nervous about all this and kept looking all around and acting real jumpy. In spite of that, things were going well until we got up around Brown's Meadows and spotted a couple of eyes in the headlights. I switched on the spotlight, Vlasak hopped out and pulled the trigger, and the animal bawled just like a cow.

"Holy shit!" I said. "He shot a cow!"

That's all old Ernie needed to hear. He floored that pickup and off we went, without Vlasak. Ernie was clinching the wheel and staring straight ahead, and we tore up that dirt mountain road like it was a highway. We'd almost made it clear to Welcome Spring when I said, "Hey, Ernie, we left Vlasak standin' there! We gotta go pick him up!"

Reluctantly, Ernie turned around and headed back. When we got to Brown's Meadows, there was Vlasak standing by the road with this gutted deer. "Ya left me!" he says, not real happy, but we loaded the deer and headed for Kalispell.

We also trapped during the winter for money. Muskrats were real easy, and I had a good trap line for them around Smith Lake. A guy could get a dollar apiece for muskrats. Vlasak had a real neat way of getting them without the trouble of laying out a trap line. He'd put on his ice skates and skate along Ashley Creek until he saw a muskrat up ahead. Then he'd get up some speed and crouch down on the skates, slide right up on the muskrat, and shoot him with a .22, which was illegal of course, but the fur trader in Kila didn't care if the pelt had a little hole in it.

Occasionally, we'd catch a weasel and they'd bring fifty cents each, and the rare mink would be worth a whole five dollars. But for me, the real challenge was coyotes.

God, I wanted to trap them mean bastards. Any cowman has seen what a coyote will do to a little calf, and I hated them, and wanted to kill as many as I could. Once when I was grown I came upon a mother cow who had tried to hold off three coyotes who were after her calf. The snow was all trampled down around her and she'd put up one hell of a fight, but three was too many against her, and while she was fighting off one or two, the other son-of-a-bitch would go for the calf. In the end, she lost out, and when I came upon her, her tongue was hanging out—she'd fought that hard—but the calf was dead. So as far as I was concerned, a coyote was a useless, no-good bastard, and I set out to trap them all.

The problem is, a coyote is also smart.

The trick is to get the coyote to put his foot in the trap, and to do that you have to lure it in, and you do that with special coyote scent. This is the whole deal, this scent, and without it, you don't have no chance. There's lots of formulas for coyote scent, most of them secret, and if you got one that worked, you really had something.

But even a scent that will bring a coyote in close don't always get the job done. I've got this friend, Greg Tipps, who's hunted coyotes all his life. One time, he set his traps and scented them, and when he went back the next day, he found a coyote had come up to a trap, scuffed up the snow all around it, and then shit right in the middle of it, right on the damn plate where his foot was supposed to go. If there was any justice in this world, the trap would of snapped shut on his nuts, and there'd be one coyote out there howling in soprano.

But no matter how smart a coyote is, the scent is still the key. I got my formula from Grandma's brother, Ray Williams, who'd been a government trapper and had the official recipe. This didn't make him real popular with Grandma, because one night Vlasak and I mixed up a quart of this scent and set it on the floor behind the stove. We had no lid for the jar, so we covered it with a tin plate. Then we got to fooling around and kicked it over. Grandma's kitchen floor was now covered with liquid coyote scent, and it stunk up the place for a long time.

This business about smell is so tricky you cannot go too far with it. Some men would even bury their gloves in a manure pile for a while before they put them on to hide the man smell, and then they'd set their coyote traps from the back of a horse, reaching down to lay them in the snow.

The most successful coyote trapper in the Smith Valley was old Hugh Galloway. He had the best scent ever, and the formula was also the best-kept secret. I do know it contained coyote piss and the scent glands of a buck deer and what else was in it I'll never know, but it sure worked. Hugh would pour some on the ground and cover it with some leaves, then set his trap on top of that and cover it with more leaves. The coyotes would get to pawing at the leaves, and bingo, ol' Hugh'd have him another pelt.

One day I saw him in Kila in his '32 Ford pickup with pelts piled higher than the cab, all tied down with ropes. He must of had five hundred of them.

But try as I would, with all my scent formulas and all my caution, I never trapped one coyote. I simply could not fool the bastards. The only coyote I ever took from a trap was one I stole from a trap of Hugh Galloway's. I and Vlasak came upon this coyote stuck by its foot in the trap, and we teased it for a while before we shot it, and then we hid it in the brush where Hugh wouldn't find it. We went back the next day and retrieved it.

So I earned my way through my teenage years putting up hay and riding horses for Howard in the summer and trapping muskrats and poaching deer in the winter. I would get an occasional job at the sawmill, and for a while I skidded telephone poles with a team of Old Al's horses in the railroad yard at Kila. But always on my mind was my lost dream of being a rodeo rider.

I would go to rodeos as often as I could and watch the bronc riders, some of them kids I knew who had made it through their early education at Burl Drollinger's arena and beyond. Sometimes they stayed on the horse for the eight seconds and sometimes they didn't, but the crowd was always with them, one way or another, and cheered as they whipped the dust from their chaps with their hats. But I was not one of them, and I watched with a sense of loss and envy.

Some years later, when Old Al was gone and I was married and running the ranch at Kila myself, I asked Burl why it was that I could never seem to get settled on a horse in his chutes before all hell broke loose and I was flying through the air. Why, I asked, did it seem like I never got to nod that I was ready before he opened the gate?

"Didn't I ever tell you?" he asked. "Old Al told me to chill you right from the start."

Hard Twist Rope

T
he years right after the war brought big changes to the valley of Smith Lake. For one thing, in the spring of 1946 electricity came to Kila. It came despite my unintentional efforts to keep it out.

Old Al had sent me off on some errand or another, and while I was riding my horse home I noticed these stakes driven in the ground along the roadside, all in a line, as far as I could see. I took up my rope and started roping them and jerking them out as I rode along. There was no particular reason why I did it. I guess I was just bored and wanted something to do, and this was also a chance to practice with the rope.

Well there I was, moseying along, flipping stakes out of the ground when Alma Conrad drove up in her car.

"Monty, don't do that!" she called. "That's where they're gonna put the poles for our electricity!"

This news brought a mixed response in our house. Old Al

was all for it, but Grandma wanted nothing to do with electricity or any other modern advance that meant spending money.

"We've got two good Aladdin lamps," she'd say. "Why do we need electricity? It'll just cost too much."

But Old Al went ahead anyway and called Howard Brist to come over and wire the house. Howard was doing fine until he hit the kitchen that Old Al and Andrew had built out of those railroad ties.

"There's no space to run wire out of sight," he told Old Al. "The only thing I can do is put it across the ceiling."

"That looks like a hell of an idea to me," replied Old Al.

So Howard ran Romex cable across the ceiling of Grandma's kitchen, and in two places he suspended bare light bulb sockets with pull chains.

The coming of electricity to our ranch opened up other possibilities that would complicate Grandma's life. The girls were all out working now, and they got together and decided their mom should have a refrigerator.

"We don't need one," was Grandma's response to this idea. "We got a perfectly good cellar."

Grandma had a point. She did lots of canning of stuff like meat and corn which she kept in the root cellar. And they had a big box of sand where she'd bury carrots. During the winter, Old Al would simply butcher a beef and hang it in the barn, where it stayed plenty cold. And during the summer, they rented a locker at the Glacier Dairy in Kalispell where they kept their steaks, picking some up whenever they went into town.

"How much is this refrigerator gonna cost, anyway?" asked Grandma.

"Fifty dollars," replied the girls.

"You just bring me fifty dollars worth of food," she told them. "I'll keep it cold."

But she lost that argument, too, just like she'd lost the one over the new outhouse.

That was the result of a WPA project designed to supply modern outhouses to our part of rural America, and we sure needed one. The outhouse we used had been on the place since the mill was operating, and it was pretty gross. Every once in a while, the hole under it would fill up, and Old Al would have to dig a new one. Then he'd hitch up a team and drag the outhouse to its new parking spot.

Well, for the cost of the material, the WPA would build you a spanking new outhouse with all the modern conveniences. They'd set it on a real concrete pad, and install a regular toilet seat, not just a hole cut in the boards, and this toilet seat was a real special one. When a man put up the seat to pee, it would be held in place by a latch. Connected to this latch was a rope that ran through a pulley screwed into the ceiling, then over to the door. When the man was done and opened the door to leave the outhouse, the rope got stretched, which released the latch, and the seat fell back down into its proper place. Those WPA outhouses were very uptown.

Grandma, of course, didn't think we needed one. But Old Al told them to go ahead, and to cut costs, he knocked some boards off an old hay shed to use as siding.

The other sign of modern times that Old Al brought to the place during those years was a car. He couldn't drive it and neither could Grandma, but all the neighbors had one they used to go to Kalispell in, and Old Al had his pride and didn't want to keep hitching rides. So when it came time for Grandma to do her big shopping, Al would call a neighbor and invite him to come along, and the neighbor would get to drive. The only time Old Al ever whomped my butt was when me and Vlasak and Freddie Cameron stole that car.

We wanted to go to a dance in Kalispell one Saturday night, but had no way to get there. Old Al was in the house, listening to *The Lone Ranger*. We had Vlasak creep up to the window and peek in, keeping an eye on him. Me and Freddie harnessed a team and dragged the car out of the shed, and slowly we crept past the house and up to the county road. I unharnessed the horses and returned them to the barn, we signaled Vlasak to hop in, and off we went.

When we got back, we just turned off the engine at the gate and coasted 'er downhill right into the shed, slick as can be and no one the wiser. Except that the frost did us in.

I didn't notice it in the dark, but there was a heavy frost

that night, and the car tires made tracks in it as they rolled silently across the yard. Even then, Old Al never would have noticed if one of his damn milk cows hadn't decided to lie down snuggled up next to the shed and not come in for milking with the rest. When Al went to fetch her, he spotted the tire tracks in the frost. When I appeared in the barn to help, he grabbed me by one arm and kicked my ass in a circle.

Old Al didn't really understand cars, and had little use for them. One time when Vlasak had a car of his own we decided to take Grandma and Al to a movie in Kalispell, for a treat, since Al loved Wallace Beery so much. We even offered to pay for the tickets.

Well, Grandma and Old Al really appreciated that and dressed up in their finest clothes. When Vlasak came to pick us up, there they were standing on the porch waiting, Grandma in her nice dress and hat and even her little gloves, and Old Al in his good hat. What we hadn't told them was that Vlasak's '35 Plymouth had a certain peculiarity that wasn't a big deal, really, once you got used to it.

The problem was the hind wheel on the passenger side flew off from time to time. This car didn't have lug nuts like cars today do. It had bolts that screwed into the hub to hold the wheel on. Well, this particular wheel didn't have all the bolts to start with, and I guess the remaining ones were sort of stripped. In any event, they worked loose occasionally and released the wheel. This was no sweat for us. We'd just retrieve it, find the bolts, screw 'er on again, and be on our way.

Anyway, this night Vlasak came sailing in off the county road to pick us up for the movie. He had just turned into the lane when that hind wheel come off again. He was going reasonably fast, so the wheel had a lot of forward momentum. The car came to a sudden stop, and the wheel shot past it and past the porch with Grandma and Old Al standing there in their good clothes. It eventually came to rest against the fence on the other side of the yard.

"Ella," said Old Al, "I am not ridin' in that three-legged son-of-a-bitch." And he took off his hat and went back into the house.

The march of progress wasn't the only thing that brought change to our lives on the little ranch at Kila, although I was slow to pick up on the most important difference between the time when I was a little boy and then. I suppose the first clue came one day during the winter of 1946, when I and Old Al were out feeding the heifers and he asked me a question whose true purpose I didn't understand at the time.

I was up on the stack forking hay down onto the sleigh when he said, "What's missin' outta that bunch?"

I looked out over the herd, and it looked like it always did, just a bunch of cows standing around mooing and waiting to get fed. I sure as hell didn't notice anything different that morning from all the rest.

"Well, what's missin'?" he asked again.

"I don't know," I replied.

"C'mon, now! Look!" he insisted, getting more than a little impatient with me.

"I don't know!" I repeated.

"That roan heifer's gone!" he shouted. "Damn it, you gotta pay attention here! Somethin' happens to me, you gotta look after her! (Meaning Grandma.) You gotta know what's goin' on here!"

I was sixteen that year and Old Al was seventy-eight. He hadn't been feeling too good that winter, which was uncharacteristic of him, and I realized later that the little episode with the missing cow was a test. He was seeing how alert I was, looking for reassurance that if something did in fact happen to him, I was ready to keep things going so Grandma'd be taken care of. I learned later that what he'd done was shut that roan heifer up in a corral before I joined him to go feed, to see if I'd notice that the herd was one short.

It hadn't occurred to me that Old Al was worried about himself, although when I thought back on it, I could see that there were signs that he was slowing down.

For example, when he was breaking colts, he worked them on the ground more then he used to before he got on their backs. He'd drive them with the long lines a whole lot longer than I remembered him doing.

And there was the incident with the big bay horse he got

as payment for castrating stallions for a neighbor rancher. This bay horse was named Rainbow, and he was a real handful, having still inside him one testicle that had never dropped.

Old Al brought him home and saddled him up and climbed aboard, and started riding him around the big corral below the barn. Well, that horse got his head and started bucking pretty good, around and around the corral, until on one circuit he hit this piece of tin that had blown off the barn roof and got covered up with horseshit.

Rainbow slipped on that tin and went down on his knees. That gave Old Al a chance to gather him up. Once he had him under control again, he hollered to me to go to the barn and bring him a piece of hard twist rope.

"Why don't you get off him and let me get on?" I said. Being sixteen, I figured I could ride anything.

"Goddamn it! I said fetch me that rope!" he replied.

So I got him the rope. This was an eight-foot length of twisted manila, rough as a cob. Old Al would double it over and use it to discipline his tough horses. He'd give it to them over and under, whipping one side and then the other, while he was in the saddle, and sometimes on a real tough one he'd raise big welts on its flanks.

"Just hare-lippin' his dink," he'd say, and pretty soon any horse that got that treatment straightened out, for the rest of that ride, at least.

Well, this day I brought Old Al his rope, and he started

in on Rainbow.

"You wanna buck, buck!" he said, madder'n hell, and around they went again, but this time Old Al knew what was coming and he was ready for it, and by the time they were done Rainbow'd had his lesson and was loping nicely around the corral, welts and all.

But I noticed that this time Old Al was shaking real bad when he got off the horse. And after that, he stayed off anything that was real rotten.

It was becoming obvious, although I tried to avoid accepting it for as long as possible, that Old Al really was old now, and that the great endurance that had carried him through challenges from the days of the frontier to the days of the Ford was failing him.

He had left the Flathead Valley at age eleven as a boy on his own and returned as a old man faced with starting over again. He raised ten kids of his own and then me. He buried a murdered son, stayed with the same woman for nearly half a century, and he forgave the brother whose foolishness had cost him the savings of his life's work.

Now his breath was growing short, something the doctor attributed to "asthma." In the spring of 1947, when things started blooming, he had an especially rough time. That summer, I did most of the work, and I counted the cows as I fed them.

On August 11th of that year, Old Al decided he wanted to

go for a ride. By then he was too weak to saddle his old black horse, so Grandma did it for him, and she brought out a chair for him to stand on as he mounted. He rode all around that ranch of his, looking over his spotted cattle and his horses and his house with the kitchen made of railroad ties. And as he rode back to the barn he had the satisfaction of knowing that it was all paid for. He unsaddled the horse and stood for a moment, looking around. The following day, I drove him to the hospital.

On the way, he turned to me and said, "Now, one thing I want you to do. You make damn sure Chet Cornelius comes to combine that grain. That'll mean some dollars for her."

The next day, Grandma sat by his hospital bed and held his hand. "Do you want me to get you a minister, Papa?" she asked.

"No," said Old Al. "If there's a hereafter, and I believe there is, He'll give me a break."

Epilogue

One day in the summer of 1972, I walked out into my hay field along Ashley Creek. It was twenty-five years after Old Al had died. I had bought the ranch from Grandma and was living on it with my wife and three kids. The grass was tall and thick, and would make a good crop of hay this year.

I got about a hundred yards out into the field when I hit water. A little further on, and I was over ankle deep. The hay I was about to cut was flooded. The irrigators had got me again.

For a while, I stood there with the water up around my shins. Then I turned around and headed back toward the road. Just then, a car pulled up and parked behind my pickup.

As I got closer, I could see the U.S. Fish and Wildlife Service decal on the door. When I came up this guy introduced himself and said, "You know, we think this would make a terrific duck refuge!"

"Well, I sure as hell agree with that!" I answered, and a short time later I became the first of the small ranchers along Ashley Creek to sell his land to the government. Eventually, they all did.

If you drive to Kila today, you'll come upon a big sign that says "Smith Lake Waterfowl Production Area." Vlasak's tire flew off his car right where that sign sits, and it rolled down the hill a short distance to your right, past the porch where Old Al and Grandma stood that night in their good clothes, waiting.

Beyond, you can see the slough grass where George the runaway workhorse froze to death, and beyond that is Smith Lake. On the other side is the road where Budd was murdered.

The government did a good job obliterating all evidence that a ranch had been there once. The brick vault that was my room, Old Al's corrals and his big barn, and Grandma's turkey house, all are completely gone.

In their place is a field of waving grass, and the marsh, home now to mallard and teal, canvasback, redhead, pintail, and ruddy ducks, among others, two species of gulls, and some Canada geese.

About the Authors

Monty Hall has been living and ranching in Hot Springs, Montana, for the past five years. He and his wife of forty-seven years, Jo Ann, raised three children, Laurie, who died in 1986, Brian, and Tracy. Monty and Jo Ann have four grandchildren, Jacob, Justin, Teagan, and Tyrell.

Monty's storytelling ability flourished during his time as the proprietor of a supper club, The Fort Owen Inn, in Stevensville, Montana. More than just a good steak house, the Inn had a roping arena where Monty and other true cowboys would show off their western talents.

Joe Durso, Jr., is a professor at The University of Montana School of Journalism. Before coming to Montana in 1984, he was a news executive and broadcaster for CBS Radio in New York, Washington, D.C., and Chicago. He began his career as a television news reporter in Washington, D.C.

He received a Bachelor of Science degree in Biology from Cornell University, and a Master of Science degree from the Columbia University Graduate School of Journalism. He served as a Test Officer at the U.S. Army Arctic Test Center in Alaska.

He lives on a small farm in Victor, Montana.